P9-DXI-080

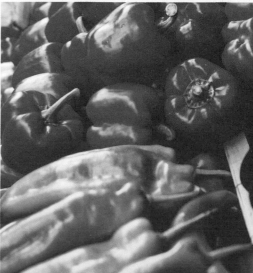

LES MARCHÉS FRANÇAIS

WITHDRAWN

LES MARCHÉS FRANÇAIS

FOUR SEASONS OF FRENCH DISHES
FROM THE PARIS MARKETS

Brian DeFehr and Pauline Boldt

Photography by Pauline Boldt

RUNNING PRESS
PHILADELPHIA

Copyright © 2016 by Brian DeFehr and Pauline Boldt
Photographs © 2016 by Pauline Boldt, except where noted
Page 21, Photographs by Bonnah Rachul (left) and Teen Gowler (right)

Published by Running Press,
An Imprint of Perseus Books, LLC.,
A Subsidiary of Hachette Book Group, Inc.

All rights reserved under the Pan-American and International Copyright Conventions

Printed in China

This book may not be reproduced in whole or in part, in any form or by any means, electronic or mechanical, including photocopying, recording, or by any information storage and retrieval system now known or hereafter invented, without written permission from the publisher.

Books published by Running Press are available at special discounts for bulk purchases in the United States by corporations, institutions, and other organizations. For more information, please contact the Special Markets Department at Perseus Books, 2300 Chestnut Street, Suite 200, Philadelphia, PA 19103, or call (800) 810-4145, ext. 5000, or e-mail special.markets@perseusbooks.com.

ISBN 978-0-7624-5915-5
Library of Congress Control Number: 2016934183
E-book ISBN 978-0-7624-6111-0

9   8   7   6   5   4   3   2   1
Digit on the right indicates the number of this printing

Designed by Joshua McDonnell
Edited by Kristen Green Wiewora
Typography: Brandon, Caslon, and Festivo
Handwritten type by 26 Projects

Running Press Book Publishers
2300 Chestnut Street
Philadelphia, PA 19103-4371

Visit us on the web!
www.offthemenublog.com

To Olenka, for not letting you steadfast love and adoration muzzle any candid cooking critiques, for signing your name on the bottom line, and for being such a beautiful anchor to everything.

Brian

To David, for your unwavering belief in me, and to Tula, for your boundless joy and winning smile. You both make me strive to be better.

Pauline

Contents

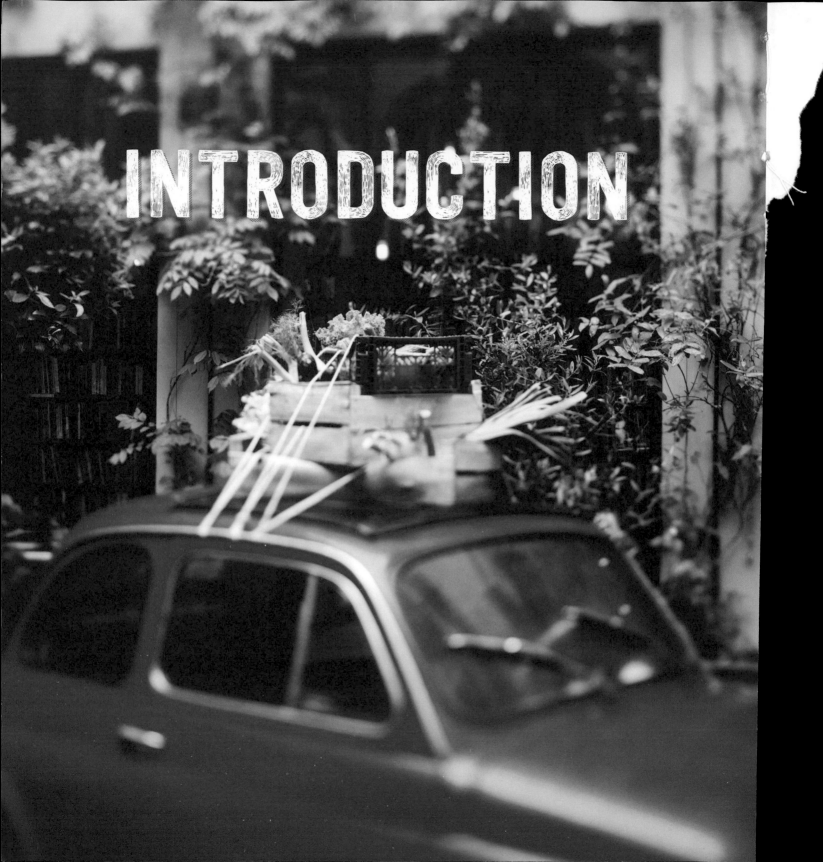

INTRODUCTION

I grew up in one of those small towns on the Canadian prairies where all the streets run in a straight line, either east–west or north–south. Everyone lived in a house with a driveway and garage and every house had a front yard and a backyard.

As almost all of these backyards had a vegetable garden, I took for granted ours, which my mother kept up immaculately. Some gardeners tend faithfully to their garden to connect with nature and bring Zen moments into their hectic lives. My feeling was that my mother's garden existed for the purely pragmatic purpose of helping feed a family of four children as economically as possible. As it wasn't uncommon to have snow in May and October, you can imagine the growing season wasn't generous, but this type of prairie folk was used to coaxing out all the land had to offer.

Since most of my childhood was spent in organized school sports, unorganized neighborhood sports, and harmless mischief, I have only vague memories of what grew in that garden and ended up later on our dinner plates. There were definitely the two large rhubarb plants on one edge; I remember because we were warned never to eat the leaves at risk of poisoning ourselves to death. And near the other edge was the dill weed that I think I got in trouble for digging up in a rare weeding job I'd been entrusted with, as I hadn't realized these plants were essential for our basement pantry's stock of pickles. Why'd they call them dill "weed" if they weren't in the same category as the dandelions I got five cents each to root out of our lawn?

Apparently we also had peas and beans, potatoes and tomatoes, and something orange—was it pumpkin? I don't recall anything with squash ever landing on my dinner plate, but I do recall that pumpkin pie was my favorite pie, and I should hope my mother wasn't using canned pumpkin pie mix. And there was an herb called summer savory. The particular flavor of this herb did manage to etch itself on my memory for life, though I can only remember one dish of my mother's that used it.

It was some kind of unpretentious and chunky soup with potatoes, green beans, and the local sausage. I loved this soup, but for some reason my mother would only cook it about once a year. It was very simple and rustic, but with an inviting mix of colors and textures. What really made it intriguing and memorable was the addition of the fresh summer savory.

My mother herself grew up on a Canadian prairie farm with a multitude of siblings of hardworking, no-nonsense German origins and traditional Christian values. One of the main goals at mealtime was to get everyone well fed, and that was my impression of the essence of our family's meals, too: all business, without any attempts at gastronomy. Besides this one soup with summer savory, I don't recall any herb or spice outside of finely ground black pepper present in any of our food. Not to say it wasn't good, but it was simple. Functional.

In spite of the culinary uneventfulness my childhood, I did become passionate about food and cooking as a university student in the big city. It was like being given the keys to another dimension of human existence when I first discovered toasted cumin and coriander seeds; ginger, chiles, and fresh coriander; garlic, basil, and extra-virgin olive oil. Just like the ever-expanding universe, as soon as I'd think I had seen the frontier, there would be a new galaxy of flavors waiting to be discovered.

I've been a private chef in the urban sprawl of Paris since 2001 and still have only three balconies instead of a garden, yet I have easy access to almost all the flavors I could imagine, an infinite variety of the earth's bounty in comparison with the family garden plot of my childhood. The greatest pleasure I get in cooking is in spontaneity and tapping into this bounty: heading out to the local food markets with nothing at all in mind for dinner, and loading up my shopping trolley with whatever looks the most ripe, curious, colorful, and tasty. Certain inspirations begin to take hold, but I resist imagining any completed dish until I return home and lay everything out on the counter and decide on the best natural affinities. That's the way most of these dishes came together with Pauline, as I cooked and she shot the dishes for this book. Sometimes she wanted to know what was on the menu for the following day; other times she was happy to be surprised when the cooking began. Sometimes we ambled about the food markets together in search of the divine and other times she was off to a café on the other side of Paris, allowing me scrounge up whatever I could find to cook us for dinner.

Throughout the book, I drew on a few classic French recipes because I believe the best cooking has solid roots, and attempts to carry on worthwhile traditions. But we've added a few of our own efforts to the mix. My father and half of my family have celiac disease and have to avoid gluten. Pauline and I decided to make this cookbook a gluten-free one not because of any mistaken idea that going sans gluten is a good general health suggestion, but rather to accommodate all those family and friends we all have who really can't eat it. The other aspect of the book we are proud of is that we've avoided the nasty refined sugars and flours that are at the core of many of Western society's health problems.

Please follow these recipes and their procedures precisely as written only if you feel you must eat exactly what Pauline and I were eating as we worked on the book! Otherwise, please don't skip any recipe that otherwise seems pleasing just because you don't have an ingredient or two that we used. Most beans can be interchanged, as well as meats, poultry, and fresh herbs. If the only fresh herb you can get is parsley, use that rather than some dried and stale facsimile of any other herbs. The point is to get something fresh from the earth and toss it in your salad bowl or get it simmering on your stovetop.

From Manitoba Prairies to the Markets of Paris

Many children from isolated rural areas end up in the world's major cities as adults, mostly to pursue work and education. Nevertheless, many people seem amused or astonished that I ended up as a chef in Paris after growing up in a little Canadian farming town. In my childhood we had the choice of only two basic grocery stores to do our food shopping, and now I'm in one of the most adored food market cities in the world. For those looking for a general lesson on how to start from nothing to become a Parisian chef, there are probably no rules to be gleaned from my story. But I will recount my story rather as the journey from starting to cook with only industrial supermarket food products to embracing fresh and seasonal market offerings.

When I moved to Winnipeg, the nearest big city to the little rural town of my youth, to start university in 1989, any savings I had from my summer job mowing lawns at Winkler Bible Institute quickly vanished the day I paid tuition and bought my textbooks. Every day I scoured *The Winnipeg Free Press* classified advertisements in search of a part-time job that wouldn't interfere with university course scheduling. After a few days and weeks I saw an ad from Goodies Bake Shop, which was in need of a delivery driver on the daily early morning run around town. It was my first big-city job application, but I got hired immediately because the boss's son, who was interviewing me, had once experienced that Mennonites were good, honest workers. I fluffed over the part about knowing how to drive a stick shift for the delivery van. It wasn't an outright lie however. My big brother had lent me his old Volkswagen Karmann Ghia for the day of my high school graduation, so I had at least twelve hours of manual shifting under my belt. Never mind that I had stalled it after almost every stop sign in town.

After some initial embarrassing driving moments and then a few weeks of successfully doing the morning delivery run of muffins, cakes, and pastries, my Sicilian boss, Ignazio Scaletta, decided I should occasionally help out on the lunch rush in one of his eateries. The first tender moments of my culinary career were spent reheating soup in a microwave and making sandwiches while two girls made coffees, served the desserts, and enjoyed bossing me around.

At the time, my apartment roommates had some of the Moosewood cookbooks, the first of which is easily one of the best-selling plant-based cookbooks of all time. The recipes resonated with me because their pure simplicity combined with an exotic international range of flavors. I felt I was traveling to distant lands for a few dollars. I'm not sure when I found the time to cook at home between work and university, but I started to make a little hobby out of cooking the Moosewood recipes. The West African Peanut Soup became one of my favorites.

After more than three years of waking up at five in the morning and rushing around the streets and back alleys of Winnipeg, and then dozing off in my university courses in spite of my best efforts, I heard one day that Goodies' most upscale location (of three) was looking for a full-time cook for the evening shift. On the menu were soups and salads, sandwiches, burgers, and pastas. Even with my previous sandwich-making and microwave experience and my confirmed reputation as trusty Mennonite worker, I was still aware that I could easily be outfought for the job by any professional cook with more than a few weeks' experience. So, I proposed to Ignazio and my future colleagues to taste my West African Peanut Soup, which was really just the Moosewood's followed to the letter, and I got the promotion from

delivery driver to short-order cook that would change the course of my life. I suddenly went from being nothing but a soup-microwaver to being responsible for nearly every soup of the day for the next year.

Probably every chef remembers the particular emotion of that first dish ever sent out from his or her hands to the paying public. It's the same pride and sense of honor of those first childhood lemonade sales, to realize that people are actually giving you their hard-earned cash in exchange for nourishment your hands have made and which they will ingest into the depths of their body. It's difficult to escape the notion of the sacred trust as well, between cook and client. Other human beings who are complete strangers to you entrust you with the task of nourishing them and giving them that which is the basis of their continued life and existence.

Culinary School in Chicago

The path I had actually been following until becoming the soup-of-the-day man at Goodies was through conflict resolution studies at the University of Winnipeg. This had been a logical progression for me because of the peace-making values instilled in me through my Mennonite upbringing. I did feel like a natural in my inner-city volunteer mediation sessions and was starting to idealize a career as a famous international mediator helping to resolve most if not all of the world's political problems. But by the time I had graduated from university, I had already worked my way through five restaurant kitchens, and I was fully afflicted with the compulsion to follow the culinary life, and my crazy kitchen colleagues, to see where we would all end up.

Since I knew Chicago fairly well and was drawn to its multicultural diversity and competitive food scene, I looked into chef's schools there and was unable to resist when the Cooking and Hospitality Institute of Chicago accepted my application.

This was 1996, back in the day when people still used libraries for a lot of their reading. I got my card at the downtown Chicago library and headed straight to the section on food and cooking. By chance I came upon *The Whole Food Bible* and some other books on macrobiotic cooking that caught my eye. I brought them home and devoured them. I was quickly caught up in the idea of healthy cooking being essential for human happiness. It seemed so obvious, but why hadn't I realized this already, after all those student meals of pork and beans eaten directly out of the can that left me so uninspired and listless? Even the prized dessert of peanut butter and jam on toast wasn't able to lift my spirits after those kinds of dinners!

I discovered a massive Whole Foods Market only a twenty-minute bike ride from my gang-ridden neighborhood, and I was in a bit of euphoria to walk in there for the first time. But how was I to afford this "luxury food" on my tight student budget? I couldn't manage it, and was forced to use Whole Foods for the occasional staple, such as the brown rice syrup that I used replace white sugar. In *The Whole Food Bible*, I learned all the grim details about Western industrialized food production for the masses, at the expense of the planet and its inhabitants. While the initial motivation may have been saintly after World War II to provide for the needy and starving as quickly and as cheaply as possible, it went all wrong after it became big business and we started buying brands on cans and boxes rather than fruit and vegetables, meat and fish.

Macrobiotic cooking espouses the ideals of the whole foods movement, but might not connect with the average Westerner because of initially being pinned to Japanese cooking and ingredients with a Buddhist philosophical foundation. But I mention it because its central tenets have formed the core of my approach to food and cooking, and because I think it's universal enough to connect fully with French seasonal market cooking: (1) following the local food availability of the seasons to deepen relationships with the nearby ecosystems and with the humans in the chain of local food production; (2) eating whole foods whenever possible for the fullest nutritional benefit, and avoiding processed and refined food products as much as possible; and (3) cooking with attentiveness and consciousness of the goal of providing yourself and others pleasure and sustenance.

Montreal and a First Taste of Market Product

After graduating from chef's school, I attempted to stay on in Chicago to work in the Whole Foods Market Café, but working visa regulations were blocking me. But after another year back in Winnipeg, working for French restaurants where most of the produce was shipped in from California and Mexico, I felt I was missing my calling. I polled my friends over which Canadian city they imagined me to be happy cooking in, and they voted for Montreal. I'd never even visited, but I gave my notice at Le Beaujolais and I was soon off on the two-day bus ride with most of my belongings to see whether Montreal really would be my cooking paradise.

I found work downtown and on the popular restaurant strip of St-Laurence Boulevard. These restaurants tended to attract cooks who were more interested in the local party scene than whether they were cooking with produce from Mexico or local farmers. My tender ideals of nourishing fellow humans in enriching environments were putting me at odds with my head chefs.

That's when Chef David McMillan came to my rescue from right across the street from where I'd been working. It was 1999 and he was already a well-respected chef in Montreal. He proposed that I come over to the other side of St-Laurence Boulevard and work at his restaurant, Globe. I started to see what it looks like when a restaurant works with local producers and interesting seasonal products. One farmer brought in those heirloom beets with the funky colors; another guy brought in crates of golden chanterelle mushrooms; another day saw a case of fiddleheads appear at the delivery door—all products I'd never gotten to work with before. Fred Morin was the genius sous-chef who had carte blanche to do whatever inspired him, so he would be off in one corner fixing up some special like stuffed pig's trotters. One day I would be blanching thymus gland "sweetbreads" and the next day I would be cleavering live blue crabs for crab soup. This was finally some gutsy and authentic French cooking, and it made every restaurant I'd cooked in before then seem like a veneer for the real thing.

Packing for Paris and its Markets

I had only just learned a fragment of what I could have learned from Dave and Fred, but through my closest Montreal restaurant buddy and his extended family in Paris suddenly came the offer to be a full-time private chef in the land of snails and frog's legs. A former Canadian lawyer and government minister was then the secretary-general for the Organization for Economic Cooperation and Development (OECD), in one of the poshest neighborhoods of Paris. He had the kind of position where one of the perks was having his own full-time live-in chef. People told me, "You'll just love shopping the food markets in Paris!" How could I refuse

myself the pleasure?

In the winter of 2001 I found myself, my knives, and my road bike arriving in Paris with Donald and Heather Johnston's chauffeur.

Donald Johnston had decided to try to sway the two-thousand-employee-strong OECD into vegetarianism. The OECD is an organization that furnishes its many member countries—and anyone else who wants to listen—with all sorts of internationally regarded policy recommendations for sustainable growth and good governance. So, hypothetically we could have been the cornerstone for a whole international dietary trend to provide more of a starring role for vegetables! The motivation was not so much to do with possible alleviation of animal suffering as it was to make a gesture in resolving the planet's issues of pollution and unsustainability of meat reliance in the diets of such a bourgeoning human population. At the same time, the famous Parisian three-star chef Alain Passard had just pulled red meat from his restaurant, Arpège, and placed vegetables in the leading role in many of his dishes. A movement was perhaps budding in one of the world's gastronomic capitals, albeit one of the most sluggish ones to make changes.

The Johnstons and I soon realized the caliber of VIP guests at these dinner parties did not allow us the liberty to be experimenting with vegetarian fine dining, and I began cooking with poultry or fish for the next five years of dinner parties. With the nearest farmers' market being only twice a week and out of walking distance, I began to do most of my food shopping in the local street market area of rue de la Pompe and rue de la Tour. There are countless such neighborhood market streets in Paris. Around this one little intersection I had access to two bakeries, one cheese shop, two fruit and vegetable shops, two butchers, and two supermarkets. I had arrived in February, and looked first to those local fruit and vegetable shops for inspiration. But even with the mild winter we were having, you can imagine there was little local produce to be found besides onions, potatoes, and a few root vegetables. I have to admit that I was disappointed. Over half of what was on display seemed to come from Spain and Morocco. Where was the food market inspiration I had been promised?

What nobody had warned me was that the large majority of the offer in the markets, whether the farmers' market, market streets, or the permanent covered markets, did not involve any direct sale from local farmers, but was just wholesale resellers who received fruit and vegetables from all around the world. You could get asparagus from Peru in autumn or winter and green beans from Kenya all year round. At some point after World War II and with the growth of supermarkets as in most Western countries, France dropped its standards of closely following the seasons and traditional food production and became enamored with the biggest possible variety of global produce available at all times of the year.

It's still the case today, although the trend is strongly back toward supporting locavore ideals. In many markets, you may only get the good fortune of having one farmer and his food represented. This is the guy to go to, to get inspiration for the core of your meal!

My first "wow" experience in the Parisian markets came on my first trip to the President Wilson market in the 16th arrondissement, my nearest farmers' market at that time. I rode my bike for about six minutes to get to it. There were the traditional hawkers of North African and Chinese descent with similar varieties of fresh but largely uninspiring produce, the flower vendor, the hat vendor, a butcher, and the bedding guy. Then, three quarters of the way through, I reached the vegetable and herb stand of the Thiébaut family, which had occupied the same spot in the market for generations. Joël and his team of ruddy vendors looked just like any other set of French workers behind their table of produce. You wouldn't have guessed by his appearance that already back in 2001 he was the supplier to many top Parisian chefs (which I was to learn only later). But all of his vegetables were such gems, and looked like they had just been dug out of the earth that morning before the market. There were so many eye-catching heirloom vegetables and fresh herbs that I didn't know what not to buy. I overloaded my backpack and my spine and bike tires suffered as I rode back to avenue Henri Martin with my prize catch. With Joël Thiébaut I unwittingly began a new personal habit of buying the produce first and then figuring out the meal from there, with the meat, fish, or cheese playing the supporting role. Correspondingly I also started to buy whatever produce was appealing, without necessarily knowing what I would do with it. Those decisions could always wait until later in my kitchen, after the prep table had everything laid out for me to admire.

By 2005, Thiébaut, the humble produce farmer, was such a star that he even had his own big hardcover book on vegetables in all the major booksellers. How many market vendors can imagine that would ever happen to them in their lifetime of selling onions and potatoes? But it was further impetus for food producers from the wider Parisian region to develop interesting and high-quality food products, perhaps first for big-budget, high-end restaurants, but also for ordinary Parisians willing to pay extra for high-quality foods. Hugo Desnoyer is another example of this trend, but in the world of meat and poultry production. His butcher shop in a middle-class, unhip neighborhood in Paris helped bring him up to rock star status by an unwavering commitment to the highest quality. Now he has three books published, and successful restaurant/butcher shop concept, and he has just opened a new restaurant in Tokyo. The peak of local food fashion is to have boutiques both in Paris and Tokyo, as the Japanese are seen as having a similar admiration for the most prized and beautiful food products.

Donald Johnston was both my boss and my career planner. After I'd been working for him for only a few weeks, he started to repeatedly ask whether I was recording my kitchen creations and when I would be putting together a cookbook. Another favorite question of his was when I would finally open my own restaurant. It was in large part because of his support that I was able to finally have my own restaurant, the Café du Port, in Paraza in the south of France, in 2006. I later returned to Paris because my wife had stayed behind for her job, and it was Donald once again who had the vision for my next step, encouraging me to launch myself as a freelance chef. I will always be indebted to him and to Heather for all of their contributions to my success in France.

My work as a freelance chef in Paris has been riddled with so many varying experiences that I feel it's the stuff of an entire book on its own. I've had the challenges of cooking for so many different locals in so many different kitchens—and shopping in so many different markets to put these meals together. As well, I've had the immense satisfaction of teaching market cooking to visitors to Paris through the Cook'n With Class culinary school and privately for Parisian tourists.

Cooking Under Pauline's Lens

Much of my work was on the fly and precious few of my concoctions were being recorded anywhere. That's where Pauline Boldt stepped back into my life at the precipitous moment. After I had already been away living in Paris longer than in any other city in my life, I heard that she was apprenticing as a photographer with both the famous British portraitist Harry Borden and leading food and travel photographer Jonathan Gregson, and was working a lot in London. She soon contacted me and suggested we start collaborating in food and photography. After only a few fun projects were under our belt based on her trips to Paris, she contacted me once from Canada with an exciting offer to put together a cookbook with her.

Since French market cooking really defines who I am as a chef, Pauline and I were both enthusiastic to build our book around this, whether it was a trendy subject or not. To me, Pauline's images seek to convey dreamy and pure sensations, innocence of childhood play, wholesome ties to nature, hope, and lack of pretension and artifice. These are exactly some of the sensations I would wish to procure with the food that I cook and the way I like to serve it. We don't spend more than two minutes styling each plate, although we're meticulous about details. With little effort, you can plate up these dishes at home with the same appeal when you try to re-create them.

Working *en binôme* (as a duo) with Pauline could not be easier, as we both are always after the same look and feel, and know how to go with the flow when beastly complications arise in the cooking or shooting. For example, one time we were clear across Paris to shop and shoot at Marché Beauvau for a dinner party afterward on the cobblestoned rue de Lappe, when I realized I'd left my box of knives and tools behind my car on the street when leaving home in a rush! It was far too late to be able to drive back through Paris and try to recover my knives, so Pauline and I had to just go on market shopping, cooking, and then serving the guests as if nothing had happened, although my insides were churning the whole evening.

Another time Pauline was to be shooting a small cocktail party I was cooking for at my own apartment. Nothing could be easier perhaps, but my first daughter had just been born and my wife and I were wrecks from lack of sleep and hadn't even had the time to clean up the apartment for the guests. Pauline laid down her camera and calmly did all the work of cleaning up the dining room and setting up all the props that we would need to make the shoot professional.

It's all in the true spirit of market cooking, letting spontaneity and a sense of fun be the guiding lights to the adventure.

Pauline's Impressions

Brian and I grew up in the same small town in Southern Manitoba. It was just as he described: small and simple, though with my being younger than Brian, we didn't cross paths as often as one would assume living in a quaint, rural town. Call it fate or call it happenstance, but we didn't reconnect until later in life in a different city, on a different continent. My husband, Dave, and I relocated from Winnipeg, Canada, to London, England, for three years. I had received a rare opportunity to study under notable industry titans in portrait, food, and travel photography. It was a once-in-a-lifetime chance to change the course of my career path and we naturally couldn't turn it down. So, we packed our bags and flew across the pond to London. I gained priceless knowledge from my time there and made friends who were just as special. I remain close with them all to this day and could not feel more gratitude for the circumstances that brought me to this turning point in my career.

There I was, a transplant from the prairies of Canada, living overseas in Europe, when it occurred to me that I wasn't the only one. Brian, whom I remembered from home, was living and working as a chef in Paris and we took this opportunity to get together. Being two small-town Canadians in the glamour of Paris, we connected over our work and ended up collaborating on a food and photography project. It was a wonderfully fun time, and the results were more beautiful than we imagined. Soon after, people began following our pursuits and we were asked to come into people's homes to cook and photograph for them. It was a great match! Nothing brings people together like food and I was there to capture the moments. A newspaper in Toronto called

The Toronto Standard loved what we were doing and published our work. Our work was so well received that I dreamed even bigger, of a cookbook. Whether it would be published was not the point: we had already realized our dreams of making a life in Paris pursuing our passions. What more could we want?

We originally treated this cookbook as a passion project. Both Brian and I would pour in our time and talents to get it done, and once completed, we envisioned it to be a limited edition that we could print for ourselves. But one thing led to another, and I found myself jetting back to Paris on numerous occasions as we worked on building content for the book. We would spend our days driving around Paris on Brian's scooter, with me on the back, gear strapped to my body and excitement flowing through my veins. Each day, rain or shine, would be tackled in the same manner; we would find our way to a market, whether a tourist spot or one of those hidden gems that only the locals knew about, and Brian would search and scour for inspiration. I would photograph him examining the local offerings, toiling with ideas in his head of the marvelous meal he could whip up. That's how Brian works. There's no preplanned schedule or list of meals. He would let the produce guide the way. And I followed along, never knowing what the next shot would bring, but trusting that the freshness and originality would lead in each frame. I think that's how most people would like to cook. You have to work with what's good and in season, in your little corner of the world. You can't spend your day hunting down an extravagant ingredient you were told to use when you have perfectly good produce available to you.

Once we found our treasures for the day, we would head back to Brian's home—a very charming, tiny little flat with a compact but cute kitchen—where we would get to work. Close quarters aren't generally desirable as we were often in each other's way, but as good friends, we made it work. With so many meals coming out of that kitchen throughout the course of the project, Brian and his wife began inviting friends over to eat the food. It was an amazing experience, fueling ourselves with recipes from the project to continue to create more recipes the next day. We would all gather and share coffee and tea and enjoy Brian's creations, which gave the cookbook a sense of community: it was bringing people together, which was everything we could've hoped for. After completing the recipes, I brought the work back to my studio—26 Projects—in Canada, where we began to piece together Brian's recipes and my photos, laying them out and designing the manuscript. It's an indescribable feeling, seeing something you've worked so hard on, begin to take shape.

Through a chance encounter with a publishing fellow, Brian and I found a path to publishing our cookbook, which seemed to excite others as much as it did us. Everything moved very quickly from that point on. It's funny how something as simple as a meal can change your life. Our passion project would be published and launched in countries across the world. We never imagined that this bucket list project of ours, a dream bred out of friendship and history, would come true. The stars most definitely had aligned to make this happen when you take into account all the facts: that we're both from the prairies of Canada and that our careers have taken us both around the globe; that we met at this time in our lives after having the same roots in the same town in rural Manitoba; that we've become such great friends and that our families are so close. This entire project has been such a joy for me, creating work that inspires me and inspires others, work that nourishes and brings people together. It's also been a great joy to eat Brian's food, but I think that goes without saying. I couldn't be happier to see this dream take off around the world, and to see where it takes us next.

WHAT IS MARKET SHOPPING AND COOKING?

Whenever I meet my students to embark on a market cooking adventure together, I usually start by explaining my vision of market cooking so they know exactly what they are getting themselves into. Everyone has the image of Parisians pulling their two-wheeled shopping trolleys around to different food stands in the market or different food shops of the neighborhood. The longer the line, the better, as to them it's usually a sign of a particularly good product. The shopping gets dragged home, dinner is prepared from that day's fresh ingredients, and the next day the Parisians start all over again, back out to the market with the shopping trolleys, looking for the biggest market crowds! There's a lot of truth to this simplified depiction of market shopping and cooking, but for me there's a deeper aspect to it, if you don't mind getting more philosophical in embracing the subject.

First, there's the activity of shopping. If it were nothing more than pulling around the trolley to individual stands and small shops rather than getting it done more efficiently with a big shopping cart in a bright, clean supermarket, I wouldn't be that passionate about it. But for me it's also the spirit of spontaneity and inspiration that counts, shopping without a list carefully prepared from an hour of cookbook recipe selections. You might know that your friends would like some fresh fish for dinner, but instead of going to your favorite fish cookbook and copying down a recipe, you just go to the fishmonger and vegetable stand and first see what jumps out at you as beautiful and appetizing. Maybe there's a lack of interesting fish that day, but the scallops are looking incredibly plump in their shells, and the price has come down since the beginning of the scallop season, so you act on your freedom to decide the main course will be scallops instead of a piece of fish. In France's fresh fig season, I often have a craving to make a starter of figs stuffed with pine nuts, goat cheese, olive oil, basil, and honey. But sometimes I've made a run of the fruit stands in the market only to find that all the figs on display are either scrawny little specimens, or overripe and good for nothing but fig jam. To really enjoy making and eating the stuffed figs, I know that they have to be really plump black figs of perfect ripeness. If those are not to be found, I hang my head for a few sad moments and then shift gears to look for some fruit that is perfect and enticing.

The same philosophy of open-mindedness and willingness to bend and adapt applies after the market shopping and when you're back in the kitchen. Not just blindly going through the motions of cooking up the ingredients you got at the market to fulfill the obligations of a recipe, but being willing to change your mind when you were sure the menu was finally set. Often the choice of fresh herbs is quite interchangeable from one dish to the next, and you might find yourself remembering how great carrots are when steamed with tarragon, when you had been planning to use it in the creamy seafood soup. Or you might realize that you bought the wrong cut of meat for the grill, and the only way it will be tender is to go for a stew. Many possible thorns lay in your path from when you start cooking until the dinner party is in full swing! You can choose to be either totally unnerved each time you get snagged, or you can roll with the punches, bearing in mind that there's always a solution. You do need to get comfortable with a few different styles of cooking and build a bit of a repertoire if you want to seamlessly cook up a menu based on just your inspirations from the market, but it's a lot easier than learning to play the piano or figuring out rocket science, so there's no reason to be intimidated.

Learning to Cook by Feel and Instinct

L et me make it clear that for the purpose of this book we're limiting our little discussion to French market cooking, although the same principles based on inspiration, spontaneity, and adaptability would apply to the food markets of Thailand or Peru. You will have the most success in your French market cooking adventures if you stick to centuries-old formulas of which foods have a natural affinity with each other. These are the flavor combinations of all the world's most famous and loved dishes. In France there are many unique regions, each with their own proud gastronomic traditions. If you simply set out to cook "French" but you muddle all of the varying flavors from these regions, you will be setting up yourself and your guests for disappointment.

To be really oversimplified, you at least need to know if you have a craving for cooking Mediterranean or for cooking with a northern style with cream and butter. I'm not one of those cooks that puts butter and olive oil in the same pan! Sure, they're both good, but so is sesame oil and duck fat. Why don't we just put it all in the pan if we're trying to get a little of the best each has to offer? The answer is that keeping the flavors in any dish as pure and distinctive as possible is the best way to convey a clear message to the senses. There is a time for complexity of flavors, such as in a slowly simmered stew, but in something like the famous boeuf bourguignon, there are not actually that many different ingredients. Plus, they are following classic traditions of ingredients melding together to produce a harmonious chord of flavors after sharing the same pot.

A brief overview of France's main regions and their star ingredients will help provide a solid base for your market cooking creativity. In France we call it "revisiting" the classics. You start with a solid foundation, which then gives you the liberty to play around with some of the ingredients and seasoning according to seasonal or market inspirations.

I will narrow down France's many food regions to the following: the Brittany and Normandy coasts; Alsace-Lorraine along the German border; the Alps and Jura mountains; the Mediterranean and Provence; the Pyrenees along the Spanish border; the Massif Central and Southwest; and everything else central and inland including the melting pots of Paris and Lyon.

Starting with Brittany and Normandy, the obvious products of reference are the fish and seafood. The most popular fish are delicate flatfish, such as sole, flounder, turbot, and John Dory. Cod, monkfish, hake, and herring are also very popular. Pretty much every kind of seafood is readily available. It's hard to think of Normandy without also thinking of apples, cider, cream, and butter, but these have become equally symbolic products of Brittany, traditionally more barren. To those goodies we can add Camembert and many other soft cow's milk cheeses, tripe, artichokes, endives, and cauliflower. This region is also famous for its crêpes and flat buckwheat galettes.

In Alsace and Lorraine, the emblematic foods often have German heritage, such as sauerkraut, sausages, schnapps, and beer. White wines are typically sweeter than those found in many other parts of France, with Riesling, Gewürztraminer, and pinot blanc leading the way. Game meats are popular from the nearby Ardennes Mountains. Wild berries are made into preserves that accompany well the game meats or specialties made from fattened goose liver. Quiche is very popular, especially the world-famous quiche Lorraine made with bacon and cream.

Moving down France's eastern border, the terrain becomes continually more mountainous until culminating with the Alps. As you can imagine, rich foods based on pork and cheese to fight back the cold, intense winters gain the greatest favor in such climates, where typically very few green vegetables could be grown. Comté cheese, made in similar fashion as the Gruyère, is the best-selling cheese in France with over four hundred competitors for top ranking. Other soft or melting cheeses work well for fondues. One of the signature dishes is gratin dauphinois, largely based on potatoes, milk, and cream. Sausages abound once again as in Alsace and Lorraine, especially smoked varieties.

The Alps go almost as far south as the Mediterranean. Coming down toward the sea, the cooking style changes most abruptly. Besides the plenitude of fish and seafood, there are specialty products, such as lemons from Menton; olives and olive oil from the backcountry; and all of the nightshade vegetables—bell peppers, tomatoes, zucchini, and eggplant—for the emblematic ratatouille of Provence. Many strongly flavored herbs are popular: rosemary, thyme, sage, marjoram, summer savory, and basil, as well as other Mediterranean seasonings, such as garlic and saffron. Provence is also well known for its mix of young and tender lettuce greens known as mesclun. Potatoes are common and popular in every corner of France, but since there is rice production in the Rhône River delta, you're just as likely to be served rice along the Mediterranean.

Following the coastline of the Gulf of Lion brings you toward Spain and its Catalonian and Basque influences on French cooking. If you were cooking with a nod to this region, you would be favoring its favorite products, such as sheep's milk cheeses, piment d'Espelette, calamari,

anchovies, chorizo sausage, wild boar, and guinea fowl, using many of the same vegetables as in Provence. This area also produces much of France's peaches, apricots, and nectarines.

Continuing our clockwise swing around France, we end up in the Southwest, which includes Bordeaux and Toulouse. In this area, duck and foie gras are king, with geese and free-range chickens just a little behind in the rankings. You also have the white bean cassoulet, wild mushrooms, black truffles, walnuts, prunes, melons, special table grapes, and sweet wines playing starring roles here. Not to mention some of the most famous red wines in the world! The Massif Central is a highlands region bordering the Southwest of France. There you find a multitude of different cheeses, such as the blue sheep's milk cheese Roquefort, and the Cantal, Laguiole, and Salers hard-pressed cow's milk cheeses. Puy green lentils from here may be the world's most recognized, often paired with local lamb.

For a last food region, I've grouped together the rest of inland France, which is of course made up of many smaller, distinct regions. The Loire Valley is responsible for most of the lettuces and many other popular vegetables in France, such as asparagus, broccoli, button mushrooms, turnips, leeks, and carrots. Fine herbs are highly valued: the delicate chervil, chives, and tarragon. An incredible variety of goat cheeses also come from the Loire Valley, as well as a lot of freshwater fish. Lyon is the world capital of French bistro cooking, which includes specialties of offal, rabbit, pike, and sausages. Just north from Lyon around Dijon, you have the world-famous mustard, as well as snails, smelly red-mold cheeses, honey, black currant liqueur, and all the famous Burgundy red and white wines.

Of course, many foods are produced in multiple regions, but having basic ideas of what ingredients are traditionally paired together from these regions will give you the necessary starting point as a French market chef to start creating dishes and menus on the fly as you shop in the market and start the prep work in your kitchen.

So, let's say you were planning to make a ratatouille, but you could only find rock-hard hothouse tomatoes at the market. Baah! You can't be cooking with those. They won't add any flavor to your other vegetables! Knowing what other vegetables are commonly from Provence, you could choose other options, such as olives or baby artichokes, or even sun-dried tomatoes. Your ratatouille would be a bit dry without tomatoes, but you could simply add some more olive oil and a little water, right?

If you were doing some delicate sole and didn't have parsley, you wouldn't replace it with rosemary or sage: their strong flavors would be overwhelming. You would, of course, choose another fine, delicate herb, such as chervil, chives, or tarragon. For other adaptations of classic dishes, you can always consult botanical origins and swap foods that are related. For example, any mushrooms can be interchanged; crucifers can be substituted for other crucifers; a variety of different onions will serve a similar purpose; dark leafy greens work well for any other similar greens—anything that falls into the same family of fruits or vegetables can usually be substituted with great success. The same holds true in the world of proteins. The flavors can be quite different, but you can still swap most common seafood in many recipes. Flatfish are generally more delicate than round fish, especially oily round fish, such as salmon, mackerel, herring, and sardines. So, you can play around with substituting different fish in recipes as long as you pay attention to the strength of flavor and the longer cooking times for larger fish. Pale meats, such as veal, pork, and chicken, can be exchanged with one another, and most poultry is easy to substitute, with the possible exceptions of duck and goose, which that have a more pronounced flavor and fattiness. Lastly, red meats, such as beef and lamb, are usually equally good with the same vegetables and sauces.

You can start to see the obvious beginnings to market cooking by instinct, but with coherence. If this talent interests you, there are some excellent books that delve deeply into the subject. Two that I found very influential good reads at the beginning of my career are from Andrew Dornenburg and Karen Page: *The Flavor Bible* and *Culinary Artistry*, the latter of which I've been waiting for my fellow line cook, Marcello, to return to me since 1999.

Saxe-Breteuil: The Quintessential Market

The Saxe-Breteuil market is the only one that can boast of having the Eiffel Tower looming so perfectly behind it. I shop at a lot of different markets around Paris and the suburbs, but when I'm shopping here, I'm usually with tourists who want private lessons in their nearby rental apartments. The postcard cliché of the Eiffel Tower behind the rows of food stands is a constant reminder that you have to pay premium prices for your peas and beans. It's not a bargain hunter's market but I'm fond of it for its wide walkways, large seasonal choice, and unharried atmosphere. The highlight for me is halfway down the odd-numbered side of avenue de Saxe, where you can find a small stand with three ladies selling a good variety of wild and cultivated mushrooms and a few specialty greens, such as purslane and baby beet leaves.

To make a proper four-course French gastronomical meal to fit the description in UNESCO's list of world cultural heritage, you will need to navigate at least five different stands in the market.

Le fromager (the cheesemonger): When buying artisanal cheeses, the cheese fanatic's ideal is to aim for the cheese made from the spring and summertime milk, produced when the animals have been out grazing and weren't just locked in the barn munching hay, as in winter. You always obtain more richly flavored and more aromatic milk at the times when the animals are grazing on grasses and wild herbs; therefore the resulting cheeses are superior to the cheeses made from wintertime milk. As well, you'll never get as full of a flavor profile from a cheese made from pasteurized milk. Cheese snobs buy nothing

but lait cru (raw milk) cheese. It's the living bacteria and its by-products that help produce complexity of flavor. That doesn't mean that artisanal raw milk cheeses have to be strong and stinky. A major factor is the type of cheese and molds, as well as the age of the cheese.

The soft, unripened cheeses, such as Camembert, Munster (not to be confused with the American Muenster, which is a poor imitation), and all of those little goat cheeses from the Loire Valley, are between one and two months old, so late spring to midautumn is the best time to buy them. The medium-firm cow's milk cheeses, such as St-Nectaire, and blue cheeses, such as Roquefort, are usually three to four months old, so late summer until early winter is their best. Hard-pressed cheeses, such as the Gruyères and Comté, are often labeled by their ages: six months, twelve months, eighteen months, et cetera. With elementary school–level math you can determine which of these would have been made with the best milk.

The cheesemongers at Parisian farmers' markets usually have a somewhat limited selection of cheeses compared with their counterparts in the nearby specialty cheese shops that you can find in almost every neighborhood with a food shopping street. In the case of this market at Saxe-Breteuil in the 7th arrondissement of Paris, the nearby rue Cler has a very fine cheese shop with large artisanal selection.

Le boucher (the butcher): In France, don't hesitate to ask the butcher for advice, recipes, and all the preparations necessary—as long as there aren't twenty people behind you in the line. I look for "Label Rouge" as a fairly reliable

indicator of high quality in meat and poultry, Scottish or Norwegian farmed salmon (wild salmon or other wild fish fall outside of the "Label Rouge" jurisdiction), and other traditional food products. Most French beef is grass fed and a lot of lean, tough meat ends up being served in cheap brasseries around Paris. If you go to the supermarket and buy the cheapest beef, you'll see in small print that the type of cattle is probably marked "Lait." This means the cattle were actually bred for milking, so you can expect to be disappointed when you sear it up and sit down with it for dinner. You'll pay a lot more money, but it's worth looking only for the beef that's clearly marked as being one of the breeds destined for gastronomic flesh-eating experiences. For example, in France some of the most reputed breeds are Charolaise, Limousine, Salers, Normande, Aubrac, or Blonde d'Aquitaine.

If you're looking for free-range poultry and eggs, the label needs to say "*élevé en plein air*," which translates as "raised in the outdoors." If the birds were raised in a cage, the labels tend not to be too proud in advertising this. The egg shells are all number coded, so if you can't read the packaging in French, the number 0 means organic, 1 means free-range, 2 means they can run around in a cramped pen, and 3 means they spend their whole unhappy lives in a cage. You can purchase good-quality free-range eggs in the supermarket for almost half the price that you would get them at a cheese stand in the market.

When buying duck, magret de canard is the breast from the ducks fattened for foie gras; filet de canard is from the ducks that are not force-fed, but still is a tasty piece of poultry. If you object to the foie gras production and force-feeding, this is the duck for you; also consider any of the whole ducks generally sold at the market (canette de Barbarie [Barbarie duck]).

Almost all the pork you see for sale today—in France as in North America—comes from feed lots where the animals are never put out to pasture. If you're shopping for the best-quality pork products with an ethical production method, it's better to insist on "Label Rouge fermier" pork. "Label Rouge" is your guarantee that the feed is free of growth hormones and GMOs, while the "fermier" aspect is the guarantee that the pigs have gotten to run around under the big blue sky.

Les primeurs ou le maraicher (the fruit and vegetable stand): It's not at all easy to buy only locally, if you also want a large selection of what's in season. Since labor costs are higher in France than in many other countries, Parisians buy a lot of produce from such places as Spain and Morocco. Locavorism doesn't have the same cache there that it does in more agricultural parts of the world. If you do see a stand presided over by an actual farmer, complete with banner advertising the farm's name and address, get in the line of eager would-be customers. Thankfully, there are now many initiatives to protect and promote the food production in the agricultural areas just outside of Paris, since the metropolitan area has been continually expanding at the expense of nearby farms.

In France you often tell the shop assistants when you want the fruit to be ripe for, as in immediately or in a few days, and they will do the selection for you. If you want to cause them to pull out their hair in rage, start squeezing the peaches and avocados to check for ripeness and put them back in the crate.

Le poissonier (the fishmonger): First, there should be a clean, fresh smell at the stand or in the shop and no odors of decay. When selecting your whole fish, look for bright red gills; bright, unsunken eyes; and a general rigidity and tautness of the flesh. For the freshest fish, simply ask what's come in that morning with a polite smile rather than a doubting smirk. No fishmonger in an inland city like Paris will try to convince you that his entire product was pulled from the ocean a few hours before you arrived. Avoid the piles of prepared fillets no matter how rushed you are, as it's very difficult to know how fresh they are, and buy only the whole fish. Fishmongers will be happy to prepare the fish however you might desire. Nothing obligates you to stand there and wait for them to finish the preparations if you're in a rush, so just tell them that you will continue shopping and will return. To avoid buying endangered species if you have an ethical conscience for our fine-finned friends, go to the Greenpeace website or others to check their recommendations. It's now also French law for the fishmonger to use the little plastic labels that show the details of the waters of origin for each fish as well as the fishing method used. Sea bass, sea bream, and salmon are some of the most popular fish in France and are usually sold both wild and farmed, with wild

salmon being much less common. Salmon is the only fish I accept to buy farmed, as the "Label Rouge" is an acceptable quality and wild salmon usually takes some effort to track down.

Le boulanger (the baker): The really top bakers—whether for bread, pastry, or desserts—open their own shops and have lines of clients at many points in the day. While the street markets are excellent for produce, fish, and meat selection, I find that the very best breads and baked goods are rather to be found in certain—but not all!—of the corner neighborhood bakeries. What's more, they have higher turnover of their goods to have optimal freshness. Ask for pain au levain (sourdough bread) and look for breads with deep coloration and thick, crispy crusts if you want any chance of rustic bread ecstasy.

St-Ouen Flea Market

Most cookbook projects have a team or a small army of people behind them. Before our most capable publisher took the reins to bring this book together, Pauline and I were a team of two. We had collaborated on a few previous shoots together, with me behind the stove and Pauline behind the lens. This time she suddenly upped the ante with an e-mail saying it was time to do a book together—and that she would be in Paris in a few weeks to make it happen!

After narrowing down our subject matter, which came about by market research but mostly by Pauline asking me, "What do you most feel like cooking?" we had to make all the other decisions. Since we were also the styling and props team, we got to run with whatever inclinations we had for the look we wanted. Besides a rare gem of an eclectic housewares store in my neighborhood, we looked first to antique shops for inspiration.

Fortunately I live only ten minutes' drive from the world's largest and most famous flea market at St-Ouen, in operation since 1885. You would have to see this place to believe it: a maze of fourteen distinct zones, some of them covered buildings and others open-air labyrinths. Interspersed among all the shops and stands are some twenty restaurants and cafés, making this market area a distinct and self-contained neighborhood. Certain alleys still give the feeling of the original flea market, with disorganized displays of bric-a-brac and proprietors lounging about on improvised seating while sharing perpetual cigarette breaks with their lazing comrades. Cross the street and you're just as likely to feel you're

in an open-air museum, each tiny and immaculate shop packed with mirrored reflections of gold gilding, silver shine, and perfectly restored furnishings fit for royalty. As one of the top tourist traps in France, there are no bargains to be found in any corner of the St-Ouen flea market. But we were undaunted and simply skirted past the golden Louis XV miniature showrooms while trying to dig up some little French dinnerware treasures to inspire the feel of the book. What we came away with was a hodge podge of silverware that we got a lot of use of and a set of quaint porcelain plates that we got less use of. Our modern, light cooking and modern, minimalist photography didn't match as well with the look of antique china, so we also shopped elsewhere. For an eclectic and more modern style of dinnerware that still has a simple, French charm, I often shop the outlet boutique, NGR, in Clichy, and Pauline adores the inspirations of Merci in Paris's 3rd arrondissement. If you do like antiques but think it's too much trouble to go out to the flea markets at the edge of Paris, there are many other interesting neighborhood options for dinnerware. In some of the side streets of the 18th arrondissement up from the Métro stop Jules Joffrin are some casual antique shops I've used for linen or dinnerware, and there's the Argenterie d'Antan near the place des Vosges for old, polished silver. In general, for high-end antique dinnerware, you go to the major shopping streets of the most posh neighborhoods, and for good deals and a lot of charmless pieces to push aside, you go to the shopping areas of Paris's more bohemian districts.

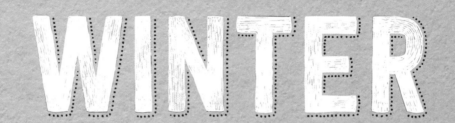

Most inhabitants of North America feel fortunate to have access to any farmers' markets at all, even if only during the summer months. In France we're blessed to have them in full swing no matter what time of year it is. If anything, a few extra stalls will be empty of vendors in mid-August in the peak of sacred family vacation time.

The onset of the wintery months is actually the busiest time for the Parisian markets, in the lead up to the food frenzy of Christmas and New Year's. At first glance, the fruit and vegetable stands look much the same as usual. But the butchers and fishmongers have copious and eye-catching displays of the seasonal favorites and everywhere the lines are longer than usual. Piles of expensive, luxurious seafood grace the fishmonger's table: lobster, scallops, oysters, crab, smoked mullet roe and cod eggs, sea urchin, and jumbo shrimp and scampi.

If you can crane your neck over the people crowded in front of the butcher shop displays, you'll find the usual holiday offerings of foie gras in many forms, black truffles under little glass domes, and all the fattened birds of the season: turkey, goose, duck, fattened hen, and capon, which is probably the most popular choice. But since it's also the game season, the better butchers carry a full variety, such as grouse, wild duck, pheasant, hare, wild boar, and venison. The tougher meats sit in a bowl or red wine marinade, ready for stewing, and the finer meats are sometimes prepared into pretty roasts with dried fruits, nuts, or lingonberries.

Note that ham and sweet potatoes are not among the options here, if you're inviting friends and family for holiday meals. And accept that the price tag attached to all this is of little importance, as it's an obligatory once-a-year chance to pull out all the stops. Then another year is rung out and dull, gray January suddenly imposes itself. There are a couple of weeks of lull at the markets as people try to get their savings back in order, and attempt some form or other of detox diets. Vendors can often be seen stomping their feet and rubbing their hands as they chat with their neighbor to keep spirits up. The only seasonal local fruits to be found in the dead of winter are clementines, lemons, apples, and pears, so we allow ourselves to indulge in the tropical fruits, such as pineapple and mango, which are often at their peak, and dream about the warm, sunny places they came from.

Starters

Lunches and Side Dishes

Main Courses

Desserts

GREEN SPLIT PEAS STEWED *with* CHORIZO SAUSAGE & LEEKS

POIS VERTS CASSÉS AU CHORIZO ET AUX POIREAUX

It's fairly easy to find split peas in France, although I'm not aware of any traditional recipes using them. Since they're not unanimous favorites among the dining public, render them irresistible with the addition of spicy sausage and a heap of vegetables and herbs. Chorizo is the famous Spanish sausage that is usually sold dried and in various degrees of spiciness. Use whatever fresh or dried spicy sausage you have locally.

Serves 4

7 ounces (200 g) fingerling potatoes

5 ounces (140 g) dried green split peas

3 cups (710 ml) chicken stock

1 tablespoon unsalted butter

3½ ounces (100 g) chorizo sausage

1 leek

2 carrots

1 teaspoon celery seeds

1 teaspoon sea salt, plus more for seasoning

½ bunch fresh chives or flat-leaf parsley

1 teaspoon freshly ground black pepper

In a small saucepan, cover the potatoes with water, set over high heat, and bring to a simmer. Cook for about 20 minutes, or until tender. Drain and set aside. In another small saucepan, cover the split peas with the chicken stock, set over high heat to bring to a simmer, and cook for about 30 minutes.

Meanwhile in a Dutch oven or saucepan, melt the butter over medium heat. Medium-dice the chorizo and brown it lightly in the butter for about 5 minutes. Medium-dice the leek, wash well to remove all the grit, and drain. Add to the chorizo and continue to cook, covered. Peel and small-dice the carrots and add to the chorizo along with the celery seeds. Add the split peas with their liquid and the salt to the vegetables and continue to cook, uncovered, for 30 more minutes, or until the split peas are just tender and the sauce has thickened. You can peel the potatoes or not, then medium-dice them and add to the split peas for the final 10 minutes of simmering. Mince the chives and add just before serving, along with the pepper. Add more salt, if desired.

LES MARCHÉS FRANÇAIS

WARM PURPLE POTATO SALAD with FOIE GRAS & TRUFFLE OIL

SALADE DE VITELOTTES, DE FOIE GRAS ET D'HUILE DE TRUFFES

There is no replacement for the foie gras in this warm salad! But I'm aware that outside of France it's not easy to get a hold of. The idea of this salad is transforming the humble potato salad into something luxurious, rich, and festive, so rather than trying to find something that resembles foie gras, you could opt for other luxury ingredients, such as lobster, crab, caviar, or scallops. You could replace the truffle oil with other interesting oils: hazelnut, avocado, or pumpkin seed.

Serves 6

7 small purple potatoes

3 small, firm, yellow-fleshed potatoes

2 green onions

7 radishes

Juice of ¼ lemon

6 tablespoons (90 ml) truffle oil

½ teaspoon sea salt, plus more for seasoning

½ teaspoon freshly ground black pepper

8 ounces (225 g) slow-cooked foie gras terrine or seared foie gras

Bitter salad greens, for garnish (optional)

In two separate pots, cover the purple and yellow potatoes with salted water and bring to a simmer. Cook until just tender, 15 to 25 minutes, depending on the size. When just tender, drain and cool in cold water for 5 minutes. Drain again and set aside.

Mince the scallions and radishes, and place them in a large salad bowl. Cut the potatoes into bite-size wedges or large dice and add. In a small bowl, whisk together the lemon juice, oil, salt, and pepper. Add to the salad and toss the potatoes gently in the dressing.

Medium-dice the foie gras and mix in gently, making sure not to smash it up. Add more salt, if desired. Garnish with salad greens (if using).

BEEF CARPACCIO, ARUGULA & AGED SHEEP'S MILK CHEESE

CARPACCIO DE BŒUF ET SA SALADE DE ROQUETTE ET DE NAPOLÉON

Probably the most common idea for a beef carpaccio comes from Italian restaurants, where it's often served with shavings of Parmesan cheese. To give it the French touch, we must use a French cheese! I love the salty but smooth sheep's milk cheese from the Basque country, but you could just as easily use an aged Gruyère or Comté. Some of the mature medium-firm cheeses, such as St-Nectaire, would also be good, but I would look for something aged at least six months, as the younger cheeses would be a little too delicate and soft to perk up the raw beef. Beef carpaccio is very popular in casual restaurants all around the country, especially in summer, but I chose to classify it with winter offerings because many people have protein cravings in the winter and not enough salads in their winter diet.

Serves 4 to 6

7 ounces (200 g) filet mignon, or more economical rump and topside

5 ounces (140 g) mature hard-pressed sheep's milk cheese, such as Napoléon, or aged Gruyère or Comté

1 tablespoon crushed mustard seeds

1½ teaspoons coarse but delicate sea salt (fleur de sel), divided

3 or 4 sprigs fresh purple basil

1 teaspoon Dijon mustard

2 tablespoons (30 ml) oaky red wine vinegar or sherry vinegar

½ cup (120 ml) olive oil

5 ounces (140 g) arugula leaves

⅓ cup (45 g) pine nuts, toasted

Save yourself a lot of trouble and ask your butcher to slice the meat for you, as thinly as possible. Otherwise, put the meat in a plastic container and freeze for 1 to 2 hours. Remove and slice with a very sharp knife as thinly as possible without tearing, and place on serving plates. Overlap until the bottom surface of each plate is fully covered with meat. If necessary, pound each slice flatter between sheets of plastic wrap, using the flat surface of a meat mallet. Cover with plastic wrap and refrigerate, if working ahead. Try to get the meat back to room temperature before serving, however, for better flavor and digestion.

Remove the rind from the cheese, if necessary, and thinly slice with a vegetable peeler or meat slicer while cool and stiff. Set aside. Sprinkle the mustard seeds and 1 teaspoon of the salt over the meat. Tear the purple basil and toss over the meat. In a small bowl, whisk the mustard and vinegar together, and then whisk in the oil. Toss the arugula with the dressing, the remaining ½ teaspoon of salt, and about half of the shaved cheese and place a large portion over the meat. Top the greens with the pine nuts and the remaining shavings of cheese.

CHICKEN BREAST, SUNCHOKE & CITRUS SALAD

SALADE AU BLANC DE POULET AU TOPINAMBOUR ET AUX AGRUMES

The most satisfying salads have an invigorating dose of acidity balanced with a touch of sweetness, and the "weight" of fat and protein. My wife is always asking for salads for dinner on warm, summer days, but salads like this can also make a starter or lunch in winter, since that is the heart of the citrus season in Mediterranean regions. The French Riviera city of Menton celebrates its lemon festival every February and the French island of Corsica supplies Paris with clementines throughout the whole winter. Kumquats are a common find in French markets although they are imported. You could replace them with a tablespoon of citrus marmalade, or simply the segments from an orange or grapefruit. Sunchokes (Jerusalem artichokes) have a long growing season and are sometimes only harvested after the first frost.

Serves 6

1 tablespoon olive oil

3 boneless chicken breasts

2 or 3 sunchokes (200 g)

3 or 4 kumquats

2 tablespoons (30 ml) honey

6 tablespoons (90 ml) hazelnut oil

Juice of 1 lime

Juice of ¼ lemon

10 to 15 leaves fresh mint, minced

1 teaspoon sea salt, plus more for
    seasoning

6 ounces (170 g) fresh baby spinach

Heat a medium nonstick sauté pan over medium-low heat and add the olive oil. Add the chicken breasts, cover, and cook over medium-low heat for 5 to 8 minutes per side, depending on thickness. The chicken should be golden brown and the thickest part should be firm to the touch but with still just a little give. Remove from the heat and let cool to room temperature while finishing the recipe.

Bring a small pot of salted water to a boil over high heat. Peel the sunchokes, add to the water, and simmer for 3 minutes. Drain and chill rapidly in ice water for 1 minute, and then drain again.

Halve the kumquats lengthwise and then thinly slice, discarding the seeds. Thinly slice the sunchokes and the chicken (removing the skin first). Whisk together the honey, hazelnut oil, lemon and lime juices, mint, and salt and toss with the chicken, sunchokes, and kumquats. Chill in the fridge for about 1 hour. This will allow the chicken to pick up the other flavors and be moist and tender.

Just before serving, toss the spinach with everything else and serve, adding more salt, if desired.

CAULIFLOWER CREAM SOUP *with* CRAB & SPICED BROWN BUTTER

VELOUTÉ DE CHOU-FLEUR AU CRABE, GARNI DE BEURRE NOISETTE ÉPICÉ

The idea of the seaweed is to give the cauliflower a little hint of the sea and marry it better to the crabmeat. If you don't have seaweed, you could replace the water with a delicate fish stock or light crustacean stock. Likewise, the crab could be replaced. Lobster or shrimp would also be excellent. You might be tempted to do this soup with some canned crab, thinking nobody will notice if it's just a garnish. When you open that can, you will want to keep your nose plugged. You can also tell your guests to plug their nose when you serve the soup. In other words, don't use canned crab, even in times of war or famine.

Serves 6

1 tablespoon unsalted butter

1 white onion

1 head cauliflower

4 cups (945 ml) whole milk

1 cup (235 ml) water

1 bay leaf

1 piece dried kombu or other seaweed (optional)

1 teaspoon sea salt

10 tablespoons (140 g) salted butter

6 ounces (170 g) fresh crabmeat (not canned)

2 tablespoons mixed crushed spices: cardamom seeds, crushed pink peppercorns, crushed cloves, and aniseeds (half as much cloves as the other spices)

Heat a large stockpot and melt the unsalted butter over medium heat, then lower the heat to medium-low. Mince the onion, add to the pot, and cook, covered, until translucent with no browning. Chop the cauliflower roughly and add along with the milk, water, bay leaf, kombu (if using), and salt. Bring to a boil and simmer gently for about 15 minutes, or until the largest pieces of cauliflower are tender. Remove and discard the kombu and the bay leaf. Purée the soup finely with an immersion blender or food processor.

Meanwhile, put the salted butter in a small pot and heat over medium heat for about 10 minutes, or until the milk solids have caramelized to a medium brown and the butter has a sweet, nutty odor.

Divide the cauliflower mixture among 6 bowls. Shred or chop the crab and top each bowl with about 2 tablespoons of it, as well as about ½ teaspoon of the crushed spices and a drizzle of brown butter.

STEWED SAUERKRAUT, SMOKED SAUSAGE & COD

CHOUCROUTE DE LA MER

This stew can be made ahead, like all the meat-based ones. Simply leave out the fish until you're ready for final heating and serving. Choucroute traditionally is the stew from Alsace-Lorraine and Germany with sauerkraut and a variety of pork products. However, the version with fish also enjoys immense popularity across much of northern France. Substitute other whole smoked fish and firm fresh fillets, such as monkfish or wild sea bass, if you can't get the cod and haddock I used.

Serves 4 to 6

9 ounces (255 g) smoked sausage

1 yellow onion

12 peppercorns

14 ounces (400 g) sauerkraut

14 ounces (400 g) fresh cod

Sprinkle of salt

3 ounces (85 g) smoked haddock

½ bunch fresh parsley, chopped

1 tablespoon unsalted butter (optional)

Heat a medium pot or skillet over low heat. Large-dice the sausage, add to the pot, and cover. Brown and sweat the sausage for 5 to 10 minutes, to render most of the fat out of the sausage. If you're afraid of sausage fat, drain it from the pot. Otherwise, thinly slice the onion and stir it into the fat. Crush the peppercorns with the bottom of a pot or the side of your chef's knife and add. Cover again and soften the onion with little or no browning over medium heat for about 10 minutes.

Drain the sauerkraut, rinsing it first if you think the vinegar or brine flavor is overpowering. Stir into the sausage mixture, cover, and continue to cook over medium heat for 10 minutes. If for some reason the stew begins to stick to the bottom of the pot, add just enough water to rectify the situation.

Cut the cod into bite-size pieces and toss it with a sprinkle of salt. Cut the haddock into slightly smaller pieces, and bury both kinds of fish into the sauerkraut mixture in the pot. Cover and cook over low heat for 10 minutes, or until the largest pieces of fish are cooked through. Gently toss in the parsley so as to not break up the fish, and add the butter to mellow out the brininess, if desired.

CHAROLAIS BEEF BRAISED *with* BROWN ALE
CARBONADE CHAROLAISE À LA BIÈRE BRUNE

Carbonade is a beef stew from northern France near the Belgian border, where beer is more prevalent than wine. The darker the beer, the richer the taste and deeper the color will be in your carbonade. I opted for an artisanal organic beer from 45 minutes southwest of Paris, Volcelest Brune, which is brewed with juniper berries. I used French Charolais beef for this, but you can use any type of beef that has been bred for high-quality meat and raised in the best conditions. Dish this up in winter with some chunky potatoes fried in duck fat or in spring with some steamed baby potatoes.

Serves 4 to 6

2 pounds (900 g) stewing beef

½ cup (76 g) brown rice flour

4 tablespoons (60 ml) olive oil, divided

1 yellow or white onion

1 clove garlic

1 bay leaf

1 sprig fresh thyme

1 teaspoon sea salt, plus more for seasoning

3 cups (710 ml) brown ale, divided

3 carrots (300 g)

1 stalk celery

¼ cup minced parsley or scallions

1 teaspoon freshly ground black pepper

Trim and large-dice the beef. Toss it with enough of the flour to coat. Heat a large sauté pan, add 2 tablespoons (30 ml) of the oil, then the beef, and brown the beef on all sides over high heat. Medium-dice the onion and mince the garlic. Add to the pan with the bay leaf and thyme, cover, and soften for about 5 minutes. Add the salt with 2 cups (475 ml) of the beer and enough water to cover, and simmer for 3 to 5 hours, or until the beef is tender. You'll have to add more water several times to keep the beef covered.

Meanwhile, heat a medium sauté pan and add the remaining 2 tablespoons (30 ml) of oil. Peel and slice the carrots evenly to about ¼-inch (6 mm) thickness. Medium-dice the celery and add along with the carrots to the pan. Soften, covered, over medium heat for about 10 minutes, or until lightly browned. Add the remaining 1 cup (235 ml) of beer and simmer, covered, until tender-crisp. After the beef is tender, add the carrot mixture to the beef and simmer until the carrots are fully tender and the sauce has thickened. Add a little more salt, if desired, and add the minced parsley and pepper before serving.

DUCK & FLAGEOLET BEAN STEW

MIJOTÉ DE CANARD AUX FLAGEOLETS

Meat addicts can often be persuaded to eat bean and vegetable dishes, as long as they include at least some meat and a rich flavor. In French cooking, meatless bean dishes would normally be relegated to side-dish status for the slab of meat! I'd estimate that half of the readers of this book would avoid turnips if they had the choice. But who doesn't love the taste and smell of duck leg cooked in its own fat?! You won't even notice the turnips, snuck in with the duck and other vegetables. Replace the dried light green flageolets with any white bean if need arises.

Serves 4

5 ounces (140 g) dried green flageolet beans

3 duck legs

2 medium-size golden turnips

1 yellow or white onion

2 stalks celery

1 or 2 sprigs fresh rosemary, leaves removed from the stems

Salt and freshly ground black pepper

7 ounces (200 g) fresh spinach

Cover the beans with plenty of cold water and soak overnight. The next day, rinse and drain, then add more water to cover in medium pot, cover and bring to a simmer, and cook for about 2 hours, or until just tender. Remove the beans from the heat and reserve about 1 cup of their cooking liquid.

Meanwhile, preheat the oven to 300°F (150°C).

Set a nonstick, ovenproof sauté pan over medium heat. Place the duck legs, skin-side down, in the pan and brown both sides for about 15 minutes. Then place in the oven and roast for about 3 hours, or until the joint moves easily and the meat falls off the bone. There will be a lot of rendered duck fat in the bottom of the skillet—don't toss it!

Peel the turnips and onion. Heat a large saucepan over medium-high heat and transfer 2 tablespoons (30 ml) of the liquid duck fat from the pan into the pot. Medium-dice the turnips, onion, and celery and add to the pot along with the rosemary. Brown lightly for 5 to 10 minutes.

Stir the beans into the vegetables along with the reserved cup of bean-cooking liquid, season to taste with salt and pepper, and bring to a simmer. When the duck has cooled, remove the skin and discard, or secretly munch on it. Pull the meat off the bone and cut into bite-size pieces. Add to the bean mixture and simmer together for at least 10 minutes, or until the sauce has thickened, adding the spinach for the last 5 minutes of cooking. Puréeing about ½ cup (120 ml) of the bean mixture will help quickly thicken this dish.

FREE-RANGE CHICKEN BRAISED in RED WINE

CUISSES DE POULET FERMIER AU VIN ROUGE ET AUX CHAMPIGNONS

Of course, at its essence, this dish is the famous coq au vin, but chicken thighs cook about three times faster than the traditional old rooster. It's even better with the addition of smoked bacon: add it or not, as you wish. I try to eat prepared pork products very occasionally.

Serves 4

2 tablespoons (30 ml) olive oil

4 bone-in free-range chicken legs and thighs (about 20 ounces/570 g total)

2 cups (475 ml) young, dry, and fruity red wine

1 yellow or white onion

1 stalk celery

3 carrots

4½ ounces (130 g) button mushrooms

1 sprig fresh thyme

1 bay leaf

1 clove garlic

2 tablespoons (20 g) brown rice flour

1 teaspoon sea salt

½ bunch fresh parsley, leaves only

1 tablespoon cold unsalted butter, plus more if needed

1 teaspoon freshly ground black pepper

Heat a wide sauté pan over medium-high heat and add the oil and chicken legs. Brown on all sides, 5 to 10 minutes. Pour off the extra fat into a second wide sauté pan or saucepan, to use for cooking the vegetables separately. Add the wine to the chicken with enough water to cover and bring to a simmer, uncovered, for about 30 minutes.

Meanwhile, large-dice the onion, celery, and carrots, and halve the mushrooms if they're large. Heat the reserved fat in the second pan over medium-high heat and add all the vegetables, thyme, and bay leaf. Stirring occasionally, brown this vegetable mixture lightly for 10 to 15 minutes. Mince the garlic, add, and cook for another 3 minutes. Then dissolve the flour into the vegetables and pour into the simmering chicken. Mix in, add the salt, and continue to simmer, uncovered, for about 45 minutes, adding water if the pan gets dry. The chicken is done when it's very tender and falling off the bone.

Chop the parsley and stir in off the heat along with the cold butter and the pepper just before serving. If the sauce is too acidic from the wine, whisk in a little more butter to mellow it.

GAME HENS ROASTED *with* ENDIVE & CELERY ROOT PURÉE

COQUELETS RÔTIS AUX ENDIVES ET LEURS PURÉES DE CÉLERI-RAVE

Before I moved to France, I thought of endives only as something bitter and crunchy for salads. It is certainly possible (and recommended!) to eat them cooked as well. The most common way of cooking them in the north is probably with cream, bacon, and cheese as a gratin. But I like them best as a cute little accent to poultry or pork, lending an interesting dimension when they've been halved lengthwise. When serving plated Cornish game hen for a dinner party, I prefer the size and presentation of a deboned half bird per person. If you want to learn, it's a useful technique for all poultry, and I would suggest checking online videos rather than written descriptions. If you're just cooking for family or couldn't be bothered with plate presentation, you don't need to debone. Any poultry you have on hand would do for this recipe.

Serves 6

6 large endives

2 tablespoons (28 g) unsalted butter

1¼ teaspoons sea salt, divided

1 tablespoon honey

1 teaspoon cider vinegar

3 Cornish game hens (about 1 pound/455 g each), or 2 chickens

1 bay leaf

PURÉE:

1 medium-size celery root (celenac)

½ baking apple, such as Jonathan or Golden delicious

1 vanilla bean, split and seeds scraped

½ teaspoon sea salt, plus more for seasoning

1 tablespoon unsalted butter

Minced chives, for garnish (optional)

Bring a large pot of salted water to a boil. Cut the endives in half lengthwise and add to the water. Simmer for about 25 minutes, or until the core is almost fully tender. Drain well, being careful not to smash up the tender endives. Heat a nonstick casserole or sauté pan over medium heat and add the butter and ¼ teaspoon of the salt. After the butter has melted, add the endives, cut-side down, and brown for 3 to 5 minutes. Turn and repeat on the other side, and then add the honey and brown both sides a little more deeply. Sprinkle with the vinegar. You can the double the amount of butter, honey, and vinegar to make a sauce to go with the hens, if you like.

Preheat the oven to 350°F (175°C). Lay out the endive halves in a single layer in a baking dish large enough to hold the 6 Cornish game hen halves. Form the hens into a bit of a cylinder and place them, skin-side up, over the endives. Sprinkle the skin evenly with the remaining 1 teaspoon of salt and roast on the middle rack of the oven for 30 minutes, or until the skin is golden and crispy. Reserve any pan juices.

Meanwhile, to make the purée: Carefully cut away all the dirty and scraggly surface of the celery root. Core the apple half and, if desired, peel it. Rough-chop the celery root and apple and place in a medium pot. Cover them just halfway up with water and add the vanilla bean seeds and pod and salt. Bring to a simmer over medium-high heat, covered, and continue to simmer until the largest pieces of celery root are fully tender. If you have any pan juices from the meat, add them to the pot. Remove from the heat, remove the vanilla bean pod, and purée with the butter, using an immersion blender or a food processor. Add more salt, if desired, or a little water if it's too thick. Garnish each plate with chives, if using.

WHOLE DUCK ROASTED *with* CABBAGE & SHALLOTS

CANNETTE ENTIÈRE AU FOUR, MIJOTÉ DE CHOUX ET D'ÉCHALOTES

The goal of this dish's cooking method was simplicity and to allow the vegetable and duck flavors to fully intermingle, without having the vegetables swimming in a lake of duck fat. For a different take, roast the duck separately without parboiling, and braise the vegetables on the stovetop, bringing the duck and vegetables together only in the dinner plate. If you substitute other leaner poultry, I would suggest to just place the whole raw bird to roast directly over the vegetables and seasonings.

Serves 4 to 6

1 large duck, just over 3 pounds (1.4 kg)

1 medium-size head red cabbage

1 teaspoon dried marjoram, or
    1 tablespoon fresh

6 whole shallots, minced

4 carrots, halved lengthwise and sliced
    finely

2 tablespoons (30 ml) honey

2 cups (475 ml) medium-dry red wine

1 teaspoon sea salt, divided

2 teaspoons crushed pink peppercorns

Large flakes of fleur de sel

Cider vinegar (optional)

Minced chives or parsley, for garnish
    (optional)

Preheat the oven to 400°F (200°C). Fill a pot large enough to hold the entire duck with water and bring to a simmer.

Meanwhile, slice the cabbage finely with a food processor, or portion it into 8 wedges and slice it finely. Select a large, deep roasting pan big enough to hold the duck and all the vegetables. Lay the cabbage flat on the bottom of the pan. Cover with the marjoram, then the shallots. Continue with the carrots, honey, wine, and ½ teaspoon of the salt.

Simmer the duck in the pot of water for 10 minutes, which will degrease it a little before roasting it in the vegetables. Remove from the pot and drain well. Salt the legs with the remaining ½ teaspoon of salt and place, breast-side down, over the vegetables in the roasting pan. Place on the lower rack of the oven and roast for about 40 minutes, removing to stir up the vegetables if you see they are getting too dry and browned on top. Then remove the pan from the oven to flip over the duck. Continue to roast, breast-side up, for another 40 minutes. If the pan is going dry, add just enough cold water to the vegetables that you end up with a thickened sauce at the end of cooking.

The duck is done when the leg joint wiggles free easily. Allow to rest for 10 to 15 minutes before carving. What I like to do with the breast to keep it moist is to remove the whole breast from the carcass and immediately place it, skin-side up, in the cooking juices/braised vegetables (off the heat, so as not to continue the cooking). When the breast is warm, it will soak up some of those liquids, but unfortunately a well-done duck breast from a whole roast duck will always be drier and tougher than a medium-rare one cooked separately. Sprinkle the crushed pink peppercorns over the duck after slicing, along with some large flakes of fleur de sel. Add more salt to the vegetables, if desired. If your wine was a little on the sweet side and the vegetables taste too sweet for your liking, try adding a few drizzles of cider vinegar. Garnish with chives, if using.

DRIED BEEF & PICKLED PEPPER SALAD

SALADE DE BOEUF SÉCHÉ, D'OLIVES NOIRES ET DE PIMENTS EN CONSERVE

You can serve this salad in winter or early spring when there are very few fresh vegetables available in the market and you're craving something different from all those root vegetables. Grilling the peppers over an open flame before optional home-preserving easily doubles their flavor. If you can't get lamb's lettuce, you can substitute any other lettuce besides iceberg, the tasteless sandwich stuffer.

Serves 4 to 6

9 ounces (255 g) dried beef (similar to Italian bresaola, not beef jerky)

½ cup (125 g) thinly sliced preserved red bell peppers (see note)

⅓ cup (70 g) pitted green or black olives

⅓ cup (80 g) thinly sliced oil-packed sun-dried tomatoes, oil reserved

1 small red onion, or 1 young and mild green onion

1 tablespoon (15 ml) oaky red wine vinegar

½ teaspoon sea salt, plus more for seasoning

4 ounces (115 g) lamb's lettuce

1½ to 2 tablespoons pine nuts, for garnish (optional)

Finely slice the beef, peppers, olives, tomatoes, and onion. In a small bowl, whisk ¼ cup (60 ml) of the reserved sun-dried tomato oil with the vinegar and salt.

In a large bowl, toss the beef mixture and lettuce together with the vinaigrette and serve, adding more salt if desired and optionally separating out the lettuce leaves as a base, for a prettier presentation. Garnish each plate with pine nuts, if using.

Note: Generally, you can find preserved or pickled peppers alongside other standard pickles in the supermarket. I always prefer oil-preserved peppers for maintaining a truer flavor than vinegar. Per pint (480 ml) of preserves you will need about 5 bell peppers. Begin by charring the bell peppers whole over the gas flame on your stovetop, grill, or under the broiler, turning to char all sides.

When the pepper skin is fully charred, but before it starts going white, which is a sign of overheating, let the peppers steam and cool in a covered bowl for about 10 minutes. Scrape off all the charred skin with a paring knife and your fingertips. You can rinse the knife and your fingers as often as you like, but don't rinse the pepper directly under water. Quarter the pepper and remove the seeds and ribs. In a medium bowl, toss the peppers with ¼ cup (60 ml) wine vinegar or cider vinegar and 2 teaspoons sea salt. Spoon them into sterilized canning jars and cover with extra-virgin olive oil, leaving ½ inch (1.5 cm) headspace. Wiggle them around with a butter knife to release any air bubbles and refrigerate up to 6 months.

QUINOA SALAD *with* CANDIED ORANGE & PUMPKIN SEEDS

SALADE DE QUINOA, DE CONFIT D'ORANGE ET DE GRAINES DE COURGE

Go ahead and multiply the candied orange recipe to have around for other uses. It's good in chocolate desserts, as well as in savory recipes with poultry, lamb, or pork. The advantage of clementines over oranges for eating whole is that they have so much less bitter, white pith. Mandarins could also work except that they have so many seeds.

Quinoa may be called the rice of the Incas, but it is now thankfully also produced in France's Loire Valley, so now I can feel like I'm cooking a real French product of the terroir as I already do with my Camargue rice.

Serves 4 to 6

Candied Oranges

2 organic clementines, or 1 large seedless organic orange

¾ cup (175 ml) water

⅓ cup (80 g) packed dark brown sugar

½ stick cinnamon

1 whole clove

Quinoa Salad

¾ cup (150 g) uncooked quinoa

¼ head frisée lettuce, washed

2 green onions

¼ cup (60 ml) pumpkin seed oil

¼ cup (60 ml) olive oil

2 tablespoons (30 ml) freshly squeezed lemon juice

1 tablespoon honey

¾ teaspoon sea salt, plus more for seasoning

½ teaspoon freshly ground black pepper

½ cup (70 g) toasted pumpkin seeds

For the candied oranges: Wash the clementines and slice finely and evenly. Discard the seeds, if there are any. Lay the slices in the bottom of a pot and add the water, sugar, cinnamon stick, and clove. Weigh down the clementines with a circle of parchment paper or a lid that is too small for the pot diameter. Bring to a simmer and cook over low heat until fully tender, about 45 minutes. Turn off the heat. After allowing to cool to the touch, remove the oranges and reheat the pot over low heat. Reduce the cooking syrup until thickened, and remove from heat just when it begins to bubble vigorously. Be careful not to caramelize the liquid; cool it quickly in a heat-resistant bowl if in doubt. Pour over the orange slices and serve immediately or store a sterilized jar in the fridge for several months.

For the quinoa salad: Cook the quinoa according to the package instructions, and then cool it quickly to room temperature in a large salad bowl. Dry the frisée and tear into bite-size pieces, adding to the quinoa once it has cooled. Mince the green onions and add. In a small bowl, whisk together the oils, lemon juice, honey, salt, and pepper and pour over the quinoa mixture. Small-dice the candied oranges and mix into the salad, adding more salt, if desired. Mix in the pumpkin seeds just before serving, to keep them light and crispy.

BEEF, KALE & BROWN RICE SALAD

BAVETTE D'ALOYAU AVEC CHOU KALE ET RIZ COURT SEMI-COMPLET

Kale has just started to gain popularity here in the last few years, and is one of the trendy vegetables in Paris at the moment. It once only appeared in the organic markets but has started to move into the occasional supermarket. If you can't get tender kale, it's better to quickly blanch and shock it first. It will be succulent, and still a vibrant green color. Trim away the stems that seem too thick and fibrous. Anytime I cook a brown rice dish, I feel I'm honoring some deity dwelling in me that is glowing with a radiant smile. This dish is my macrobiotic side just slightly overcoming my classic French tendency for half a day.

Serves 6

¾ cup (140 g) uncooked short-grain
   brown rice

2 cups (475 ml) water

1 teastoon sea salt, plus more for salting
   water and seasoning

13 ounces (370 g) flank steak

1 tablespoon peanut oil

1 sprig fresh dill or rosemary, minced

6 ounces (170 g) young, tender kale

4 ounces (115 g) button mushrooms

2 green onions

1 medium-size cucumber dill pickle, such
   as Kirby

½ cup (120 ml) olive oil

2 tablespoons (30 ml) sherry vinegar

Rinse the rice, add to a saucepan with the water, salt lightly, and bring to a boil. Cover and simmer over low heat for 25 minutes or according to the package instructions. When all the water has been absorbed, remove the rice from the heat and allow it to finish puffing up and drying while covered. Then uncover and fluff it up with a fork. Cool the rice down more quickly in a large salad bowl.

If the meat is wet, dry it with paper towels. Rub it with the peanut oil. Heat a nonstick sauté pan or cast-iron skillet and place the meat in the pan when it's hot enough to sizzle. Sear the meat over medium-high heat for about 2 minutes per side for rare/medium-rare, depending on the thickness. Remove from the heat and allow to rest for 10 minutes before medium-dicing. Add 1 teaspoon of the salt and the dill.

Mince the kale, mushrooms, green onions, and pickle. Place in the salad bowl with the rice; add the olive oil, vinegar, and cooked steak; and toss, seasoning with more salt, if desired.

ROASTED ONIONS STUFFED with GREEN LENTILS

OIGNONS DOUX RÔTIS ET FARCIS AUX LENTILLES VERTES

If you want to serve these as a lunch main course, an optional side could be some tender kale leaves, parboiled for three minutes and then sautéed with a little olive oil. This dish is as close as I was willing to go to honor Pauline's request to include French onion soup in this book! Many of the flavors of the classic soup are there, but in a completely different form, along with the addition of lentils for the extra protein.

Serves 6

6 large sweet onions

½ teaspoon sea salt, plus more as needed

1 bay leaf

1 tablespoon minced fresh thyme, or 1 teaspoon dried

1 cup (210 g) dried green lentils

3 cups (710 ml) beef, chicken, or vegetable stock

2 tablespoons (5 g) minced fresh summer savory

1 teaspoon freshly ground black pepper

3 tablespoons (45 ml) walnut oil

1 teaspoon sherry vinegar

2 ounces (55 g) grated Gruyère cheese

Minced chives, for garnish

Trim as little of the root of the onions as possible. Cut off the top third of the onions, reserving the onion tops in the fridge for another recipe. Without peeling, place the onions in a large pot and cover with salted water. Add the bay leaf and thyme and bring to a boil. Lower the heat and simmer for 45 to 60 minutes, or until the onions are fully tender when pierced with a paring knife in the center. Drain and let the onions cool to the touch.

Meanwhile, in a medium pot, bring the lentils to a simmer over medium heat with the stock and summer savory, and gently cook, covered, for about 25 minutes or according to the package instructions. The lentils should be tender but not mushy, as they will continue to cook in the onions. While the lentils are still hot, stir in the ½ teaspoon salt, pepper, oil, and vinegar.

Preheat the broiler at about 400°F (200°C). Hollow out the onions carefully, using a grapefruit spoon or melon baller. You will need to leave two or three outer layers of each onion intact so that it doesn't collapse. Dice up the insides of the onion that you just removed and mix into the lentils. Sprinkle a little more salt over the hollowed onions and fill them generously with the lentils.

Place the onions in a baking dish and broil in the middle of the oven for about 15 minutes. Remove, top them with the grated cheese, and continue to broil on the top rack of the oven until the cheese browns. Serve, spooning any cooking liquid over each onion. Garnish each plate with chives.

LEMON, HONEY & RASPBERRY TARTLETS

TARTELETTES AU CITRON AVEC MIEL ET FRAMBOISES

When I first moved to France, I had Patricia Wells's cookbook on Provence cooking and I loved her lemon pie recipe, making it regularly for dinner parties. I've never strayed too far from this recipe, and certainly not the technique, which involves only a stovetop cooking of the lemon curd. This then sets in the prebaked tart shell while cooling, which results in a much more moist and silky lemon filling than the ones that are baked. My own variation here is replacing white sugar with honey in the lemon curd, and with dark brown sugar for the crust. Much healthier than meringue, raspberries are the other go-to topping in France. An alternative to sprinkling icing sugar is to finely grate some egg white meringues onto the raspberries.

Gluten-free pastry will always be unworkable and crumble up when serving if you simply substitute such flours as rice or potato. The best results will be achieved when you use store-bought or home blends of multiple gluten-free flours, usually including some gums that replace the elasticity that gluten offers. If you are accustomed to using wheat flours, you can replace this book's gluten-free flours with whole wheat pastry flour. The shortbread pastry will also make one 10-inch/25-cm tart: double the amount of filling for a single large tart.

Makes 7 (4-inch/10 cm) tartlets

SWEET SHORTBREAD PASTRY:

9 ounces (255 g) gluten-free all-purpose or bread flour, plus more if needed

3 ounces (85 g) dark brown sugar, plus more for dusting

1 ounce (28 g) ground almond meal

½ cup (113 g) unsalted butter, at room temperature, plus more for pans

1 large egg, lightly beaten

LEMON CURD:

2 large eggs

3 large egg yolks

7 ounces (200 ml) honey

Grated zest and juice of 2 lemons

½ cup (113 g) unsalted butter, at room temperature, cubed

TOPPING:

1 cup (237 ml) raspberry or almond liqueur (optional)

1 pound (455 g) fresh raspberries

Confectioners' sugar, for sprinkling

To make the pastry dough: Put all of the ingredients in a food processor, in the order given. Let the machine run until the ingredients clump together and you obtain a ball. If the dough sticks to the blade or your fingers, add another spoon or two of flour and incorporate fully. Wrap the ball of dough in plastic wrap and refrigerate for at least 1 hour.

Preheat the oven to 400°F (200°C).

Bring the dough back to near room temperature so it will be pliable. Butter 7 nonstick tartlet pans and dust with brown sugar. Roll the dough into a cylinder and cut it into 7 equal portions, about 1.7 ounces (48 g) each. Use your thumbs to press the dough evenly into the bottom of the prepared pans, and then from the center, push the dough with your thumbs toward the sides until the dough comes up just above the edge of each pan. Poke all over with a fork to keep the pastry flat while baking. Alternatively, roll out the entire amount of dough on a flat surface, then cut out circles slightly larger than the diameter of your tartlet pans and press lightly each circle of dough into place in the pans. (Keep in mind that the gluten-free dough is usually more fragile and crumbly, which makes this latter, traditional technique trickier.) Bake in the lower third of the oven for 10 to 12 minutes or until kissed light brown around the edges and in the center. Remove from the oven, let cool, and carefully remove from the pans.

To make the lemon curd: Beat all the eggs and egg yolks, honey, and lemon juice and zest with a whisk in medium saucepan or sauté pan. (Nonstick pans make the washing-up easier afterwards when the egg mixture has dried on.) Whisk constantly over low heat until light, creamy, and thickened, but without any solid bits, 5 to 7 minutes. Initially steam will begin to rise from the mixture. When the eggs are cooked enough, you will see traces of the pan bottom with each whisking motion. Immediately remove from the heat if you ever see traces of solid egg. An instant-read thermometer should read 165°F (74°C), if you should choose to use one. Remove from the heat and whisk in the butter in about eight additions.

Use a spatula to scrape the mixture into a stainless-steel bowl to stop the cooking. Chill for 5 minutes while occasionally whisking to cool it down. Then pour into the cooked and cooled tartlet shells, let cool to room temperature on the countertop, and refrigerate to set for at least 2 hours.

To make the topping: reduce the liqueur in a small pot until syrupy, and drizzle around each plate. Just before serving, arrange the raspberries across the top and sprinkle with confectioners' sugar.

CHILLED DARK CHOCOLATE TERRINE *with* CANDIED CLEMENTINES

TERRINE AU CHOCOLAT NOIR CUITE À LA VAPEUR, CONFIT DE CLEMENTINES

The best time for clementines is in the winter, but you can still find them in early spring, when so little other fresh fruit is available. Cases upon cases of Spanish clementines flood the market stalls from October throughout the winter, but the most prized ones come from Corsica for a much shorter time. Replace them with mandarins, which are actually more fragrant, or even seedless oranges. I prefer buying organic for this because a lot of conventional citrus skin has absorbed a lot of chemical sprays before harvest, and sometimes after as well.

Serves 6

TERRINE:

½ cup (115 g) unsalted butter, plus 2 tablespoons (28 g) for pan

7 ounces (200 g) dark chocolate (60% to 70% cacao)

⅓ cup (80 ml) heavy whipping cream

5 large eggs, at room temperature, separated

¾ cup (150 g) packed dark brown sugar

Dark chocolate curls, for garnish (optional)

CANDIED CLEMENTINES:

4 clementines, preferably organic and seedless

1¾ cups (415 ml) water

1 cup lightly packed dark brown sugar (7 ounces/200 g)

2 whole cloves

1 stick cinnamon

For the terrine: Preheat the oven to 300°F (150°C) on the convection setting (or to 325°F/165°C if you don't have one). Boil a kettle of water and pour it into a pan in the bottom of the oven to create steam, or use your oven's steam setting. Melt or soften the 2 tablespoons (28 g) of butter and use it to butter a medium, rectangular or half-cylindrical loaf pan or terrine dish. Line the buttered pan with enough plastic wrap to pull some excess wrap over all the edges and with as little air as possible trapped between the wrap and the pan.

Place the chocolate and the remaining ½ cup (115 g) of butter in a heatproof bowl that fits into a small pot without touching the bottom, to create a double boiler. Bring about 1 inch (2.5 cm) of water to a simmer in this pot and allow the steam to melt the chocolate in the bowl, stirring every 2 minutes. As soon as the chocolate is fully melted, carefully remove the bowl from the pot and stir in the cream.

Meanwhile, separate the eggs, placing the whites in an electric mixer bowl or other large bowl and the yolks in a separate large bowl. Add about three quarters of the sugar to the yolks and beat with a whisk for 1 minute. Then whisk the warm chocolate mixture into the egg yolks and set aside.

Begin beating the egg whites on medium speed for about 2 minutes before increasing the speed to high. Beat until you obtain medium-firm, moist peaks. Add the remaining sugar and continue beating until you have stiff, moist peaks, stopping before the egg whites begin to get lumpy or grainy.

Fold the whites into the chocolate, one quarter at a time. Trouble yourself to get the mixture homogenous only on the final addition of egg white; don't overmix. When there are no little clumps of egg white remaining,

pour the batter into the prepared loaf pan, which can be filled anywhere from half to three-quarters full. Place in the bottom third of the oven. It's not necessary for the loaf pan to be sitting directly in the steam bath. Bake for about 70 minutes, or until a knife inserted into the center comes out clean.

Meanwhile, to candy the clementines: Wash the clementines and slice them evenly to about a pencil's width (5 mm) thickness, discarding any seeds that you find. Lay the slices in the bottom of a large pot and add the water, sugar, cloves, and cinnamon stick. Keep the clementines submerged with a circle of parchment paper or a lid just smaller than the pot diameter. Bring to a simmer over low heat and cook until fully tender, about 45 minutes. Turn off the heat and allow to cool to room temperature, then remove the clementine slices, reheat the pan over low heat, and reduce the cooking syrup until thickened, or to just when it all begins to bubble frenetically. Be careful not to caramelize the liquid; remove it from the heat and pour it quickly into a bowl to cool, if in doubt. Pour this syrup back over the clementine slices and serve immediately or store in the fridge a few weeks in a sterilized canning jar.

Cool the chocolate terrine to room temperature after baking. While this dessert can be served immediately, I prefer to chill it for at least 2 hours or overnight and serve it cool. Invert carefully onto a rectangular or round serving plate. A fully flat plate will give you the option of slicing with a cheese wire, which is less messy than having to use a hot, wet knife. Serve with about 3 wedges of clementine per serving and some chocolate curls, if using.

Spring is of course the time of hope, transformation, and budding new energy. It's also many people's favorite time to visit Paris, with everything green and fresh and the air invigorating. With the blooming cherry blossoms and magnolias, even the dourest Parisians can become lighthearted. I recall marveling at the surprising changes in weather during my first April living here. There were so many days of bright blue skies full of cheer, but when I had stepped back out of the cheese shop I would find myself in the middle of a torrential downpour. Everyone in the markets would be running for cover to the stalls with the biggest awnings and the vendor selling umbrellas and rain jackets would be doing a brisk business. I might run into a café to dry out and warm up with an espresso, and by the time I had steeled myself to face the weather, I would emerge to find the sun blazing more intensely than ever as it reflected off all the wet cobblestones and bright Haussmannian apartment blocks. The umbrella vendor is usually smart enough to be selling sunglasses as well.

Winter is neither harsh nor long in the north of France, but at the official start of spring near the end of March, Parisians won't find an abundance of local fruits in the market; it's mostly still the winter vegetables. But the Easter holiday approaches, so there's expectancy to find an early plethora of baby vegetables to accompany family holiday dinners. You'll find even more than the usual displays of bunches of tender little vegetables still bearing their green shoots: onion, radish, carrot, turnip, and beets. The tiny (grenaille) potatoes have already been dug from the earth. The little artichokes sold in a bunch of five make their appearance, as well as the freshest bunches of watercress.

Easter in countries of Catholic tradition is a time to reflect on sacrifice and resurrection. The butcher focuses on the aspect of sacrifice, with special attention to those youngest and most innocent: suckling pig, lamb, young goat, and milk-fed veal. After Easter, the Sunday roast chicken quickly regains its eminent position. As May approaches we finally discover some of the season's jewels appearing in the market, stirring the passion of cooks and chefs a little more than baby turnips. For example, the prized green asparagus from Pertuis in Provence, the perfect and tender Gariguette strawberries from Brittany, and morels, my personal favorite mushroom. By the end of spring, the fruit and vegetable shops and stalls have reached one of the pinnacle points of the year, with all their little *barquettes* (baskets) of fresh berries, thick hulks of white asparagus ready for braising, and all that is green and life-giving: peas in the pod, slender beans, and pots of every herb from sorrel to tarragon.

Starters

Main Courses

Lunches and Side Dishes

Desserts

ARTICHOKE, SCALLOP & BABY ROMAINE SALAD

SALADE AUX ARTICHAUTS, AUX NOIX DE ST-JACQUES ET À LA SUCRINE

In the off chance that you can't get scallops but do have baby octopus and a grill, the salad will be at least as good, if not better! You can replace the baby artichokes with wedges of large globe artichoke; they just won't be as pleasing to the eye, and you'll need a very sharp chef's knife or bread knife to trim off the green parts. Don't throw the whole lemon with rind into your simmering artichokes as it will only increase their natural bitterness. Sometimes I reserve a couple of tablespoons of the artichoke poaching liquid and whisk it into my vinaigrette.

Serves 4

IMPROVISED POACHING STOCK:

4 cups (945 ml) water

1 onion of any variety

1 clove garlic

1 carrot, rough-chopped

1 stalk celery, rough-chopped,
    or 1 tablespoon celery seeds

1 bay leaf

Juice of ½ lemon, or 2 tablespoons
    (30 ml) white wine vinegar

1 tablespoon sea salt

8 baby artichokes (poivrades)

SALAD:

8 to 12 large fresh scallops, depending
    on how generous you want to be

2 or 3 heads baby romaine lettuce

2 leaves radicchio

¼ cup (60 ml) plus 1 tablespoon olive oil,
    divided

1 teaspoon sea salt, divided

2 tablespoons (30 ml) freshly squeezed
    lemon juice

¼ cup (15 g) minced fresh parsley or
    chives

To make the stock: Combine the water, onion, garlic, carrot, celery, bay leaf, lemon juice, and salt in a medium pot.

Tear off all the green leaves from the artichokes with your fingers and trim away any remaining green surface with a paring knife. Scoop and scrape out the choke with a teaspoon. Quarter or halve the artichokes, depending on what you feel is bite-size, and place the artichoke pieces in the pot. Bring to a boil and then lower the heat to simmer for 15 to 20 minutes, or until a paring knife easily penetrates the thickest pieces. Remove from the heat and allow to cool to room temperature in the poaching liquid, then drain.

To make the salad: Clean and trim the scallops, lettuce, and radicchio, if needed. Heat a medium nonstick sauté pan, add 1 tablespoon of the oil, and sear the scallops over medium-high heat for about 2 minutes per side. Sprinkle with ½ teaspoon of the salt and transfer them to a large bowl to cool to room temperature. If the scallops are large, halve them and add them back to the bowl with the artichokes. Tear the lettuce leaves, slice the radicchio, and add them to the bowl. Whisk the remaining ¼ cup (60 ml) of oil and the lemon juice with the remaining ½ teaspoon of salt and parsley and toss with the salad.

EGG, SMOKED BACON & FRISÉE SALAD

SALADE FRISÉE AUX ŒUFS DURS ET À LA POITRINE FUMÉE

In my mind, this is the perfect Saturday lunch salad when the weather has turned cold and you've slept in after a Friday night party. You can also think of it as an egg and bacon sandwich where the bread's been replaced with potato. Potato salad may seem like a purely North American picnic dish, but it could also be found at some trendy little lunch spot in Paris, where a lot of American diner influences have been riding a wave of popularity for the last few years. The smoke in the bacon adds a touch of sophistication.

Serves 4 to 6

3 medium-size, firm yellow-fleshed or waxy potatoes

½ teaspoon sea salt, plus more as needed

12 strips smoked bacon

6 large eggs

4 ounces (115 g) frisée lettuce, washed and dried well

½ cup (115 g) plain yogurt

1 tablespoon white wine vinegar or freshly squeezed lemon juice

⅓ cup (20 g) minced fresh parsley

½ teaspoon freshly ground black pepper

In a medium pot, cover the potatoes with salted water and bring to a boil. Simmer until just tender. A toothpick should insert easily into the thickest potato. Drain and set aside.

Cook the bacon in a nonstick pan over medium heat for 6 to 8 minutes, or until browned and crispy. Remove from the pan and cool on paper towels to absorb the excess fat.

Place the eggs in a single layer in the bottom of a pot, cover fully with cold water, and bring to a boil. Remove from the heat as soon as the water boils. Cover with a tight-fitting lid and allow to slowly cook off the heat, which helps prevent the green sulphuric layer from forming between the yolk and the white. After 12 minutes, drain and rinse with cold water for 1 minute, crack the shells gently all around, and peel while still warm.

Medium-dice the potatoes and bacon. Cut the eggs into wedges. Break the frisée into bite-size pieces and place all these ingredients in a large salad bowl.

In another bowl, mix the yogurt, vinegar, parsley, ½ teaspoon salt, and pepper. Toss in with the salad, add more salt, if desired, and serve at room temperature or slightly chilled.

SCALLOPS & ASPARAGUS *with* LEMON MOUSSELINE SAUCE

NOIX DE ST-JACQUES ET ASPERGES VERTES EN SAUCE MOUSSELINE AU CITRON

Mousseline sauce is an old French classic that will horrify those afraid of butter, eggs, and cream. It's basically a hollandaise sauce that is "lightened" by the addition of whipped cream at the end of cooking! Adding lots of fresh herbs keeps rich sauces balanced and gives them a little veneer of healthiness.

Serves 6

1 cup (225 g) unsalted butter

ASPARAGUS:

18 green asparagus spears, trimmed

Grated zest of 1 lemon

Grated zest of 1 orange

Grated zest of 1 lime

Sea salt, for salting water and seasoning

LEMON MOUSSELINE SAUCE:

5 large egg yolks

5 tablespoons (75 ml) water

Juice of ½ lemon

¾ cup (175 ml) cold heavy whipping cream

1 teaspoon sea salt

½ teaspoon freshly ground black pepper

SCALLOPS:

18 fresh, plump scallops , with or without their coral

2 tablespoons minced fresh chives

2 tablespoons minced fresh chervil or parsley

1 teaspoon sea salt

1 tablespoon unsalted butter

Start by clarifying the butter: Heat it gently in a small pot, skimming off and discarding any milk solids that rise to the top. Set the clarified butter aside to cool to room temperature.

To make the asparagus: Bring a large pot of salted water to a boil and add the asparagus. Depending on the thickness, simmer them 2 to 4 minutes, or until just cooked through. When you pick them up from their center, they will bend slightly but readily. They're overcooked if they bend completely Drain well and toss with the citrus zests. Keep warm in a very low oven, sprinkling with more salt, if desired.

Start the mousseline sauce: Place the egg yolks, water, and lemon juice in either a medium, heavy-bottomed sauté pan or a small, heavy-bottomed pot. Whisk well and heat over low heat for about 5 minutes while whisking continuously. Initially some steam will start to rise from the pan and then the eggs will thicken enough that you see traces of the pan visible with each stroke of the whisk. If you're using a thermometer, the eggs will be done at 165°F (74°C). If ever you see traces of fully coagulated egg that resemble scrambled eggs, immediately remove from the heat and add a splash of water to cool the mixture. Slowly whisk in the clarified butter off the heat. Strain if necessary to remove any overcooked egg, and transfer the sauce from the hot pan to a medium bowl.

Meanwhile, beat the cream in a cold bowl until it has medium-stiff peaks. Fold into the egg mixture and keep near the warm stovetop but not directly on the heat, which will cause it to separate.

To make the scallops: Rinse and dry the scallops and then toss them with the minced herbs and salt. Heat a large nonstick sauté pan and melt the butter. Then add the scallops without allowing them to touch one another. Cover and cook over low heat for 2 minutes each side and with as little browning as possible, or until cooked medium-well and still a little translucent in the center.

Plate 3 asparagus spears and 3 scallops per person and spoon some warm but not hot mousseline sauce alongside. You can serve this a little hotter if you preheat the plates in the microwave or a low oven.

SOLE FILLET STUFFED with WATERCRESS & CHIVES
ROULEAUX DE SOLE FARCIS AU CRESSON ET À LA CIBOULETTE

Since each sole (or other varieties of flatfish) has four fillets, you will get twelve fillets from three fish, which results in two fillets per person if there are six of you at the table. If you want to turn this into a main course, either add another fillet per person or use slightly larger fish. As an alternative to stovetop cooking, you can also bake these fish rolls in the oven at 325°F (165°C) adding at least five minutes to the cooking time. Spinach or sorrel would be a perfect alternative to the watercress. If using spinach, I would use about four ounces (115 g), cooking it down a little in a sauté pan before rolling it up in the fish. Serve with some crusty baguette to soak up the sauce, and some boiled green beans topped with sesame seeds.

Serves 6

3 medium-size sole or other fresh medium-size flatfish, such as flounder or plaice, filleted and skinned, the bones from 1 or 2 fish reserved for the sauce (ask your fishmonger to do this for you)

3 carrots, divided

1 yellow or white onion or leek

1 stalk celery

1 bay leaf

2 sprigs fresh thyme

½ cup (120 ml) dry white wine

6 cups (1.4 L) water

¾ cup (175 ml) heavy whipping cream

½ teaspoon sea salt, divided

½ bunch fresh chives, minced

24 sprigs plus ¼ cup (20 g) leaves fresh watercress, divided

1 small zucchini, cut into 36 matchsticks as long as the widest part of the fish fillets

Rinse the reserved fish bones and place them in a wide saucepan. Add 1 of the carrots, the onion, celery, bay leaf, thyme, wine, and water, and bring to a boil. Without discarding the herbs, skim off whatever scum floats to the top of the pot at the initial boiling. Continue simmering until the stock has reduced to ½ to ¾ cup (120 to 175 ml) of liquid. Strain the sauce through a colander and discard the solids. Add the cream to the stock and place back over the heat in a medium pot at a gentle simmer, to thicken.

Cut the remaining carrots into fine dice (brunoise). Place them in a single layer in a large pot and just cover with water. Bring to a simmer over medium heat and soften until the pot is almost dry but the carrots aren't sticking to the bottom. Transfer the carrots to a bowl.

Lay out all the fish fillets with the thicker head end away from you, and the grayer or less pretty-skinned side facing you. Almost all skinned fillets have a prettier, pearly side and a less presentable side where the skin was, which is more discolored. The idea is to have the prettier side showing after rolling, and the "uglier" side hidden on the inside of the roll. Pat the fish dry with a paper towel if it is wet. Season with ¼ teaspoon of the salt and scatter the chives and the brunoise of carrot over the surface. Take 2 little sprigs of watercress and 3 zucchini matchsticks per fillet and place perpendicular to the fish near the tail end of the fish. Starting from the tail end, roll the fish around the watercress and keep rolling all the way to the thickest part. Stand up the roll on end and pierce a toothpick through the center to hold it all together. The watercress should be visible in the center of the roll. Make sure the thickest part of the fillet is not what you attempt to roll into the center of the roll, or it will likely be raw or the outside of the fish extremely overcooked. Repeat with the remaining fillets.

Pour about half of the sauce into a wide saucepan large enough to hold all the fish without crowding. Add the fish, standing up each roll with its thickest part on the bottom, and place the pan, covered, over medium heat to start. As soon as the sauce begins to simmer, lower the heat to the gentlest simmer and continue to cook, covered, for about 10 minutes, which may vary according to the size of your fish. The thickest parts will feel firm to the touch when cooked.

While the fish is cooking, add the remaining watercress leaves and the remaining ¼ teaspoon of salt to the remaining sauce and simmer for 3 minutes more. Purée the sauce with an immersion blender.

Remove the cooked fish from the pan and add the cooking liquid to the pot of finished sauce. Pull the toothpicks from the fish before serving, unless it's for close family!

CREAMY SHRIMP SALAD with CUCUMBER & RADISH

SALADE AUX CREVETTES, AU CONCOMBRE ET AU RADIS

Lemon balm isn't the easiest herb to find in the markets, but it's as easy to grow on your balcony or in your garden as mint, to which it is a cousin. Lemon balm adds a mild lemongrass flavor without getting into some dubious fusion cooking. You would be equally happy just going with mint instead of lemon balm, but I just wanted to use what was growing on my balcony.

Serves 6

1½ teaspoons olive oil

18 large raw shrimp, peeled, shells reserved

¼ teaspoon piment d'Espelette or cayenne pepper

1¼ teaspoons sea salt, divided, plus more for salting water and seasoning

20 radishes, trimmed

7 mini-cucumbers, or 1½ English cucumbers

½ red onion

30 leaves fresh lemon balm, or 20 leaves fresh mint

½ cup (120 g) crème fraîche or full-fat Greek yogurt

½ teaspoon finely ground black pepper

OPTIONAL SAUCE FOR PLATING:

½ cup (120 ml) Muscat or white Porto

Shrimp shells

Grated zest and juice of 1 orange

Pinch of piment d'Espelette or cayenne pepper

Pinch of sea salt

Heat a large sauté pan over medium-high heat and add the oil. Add the shrimp, piment d'Espelette, and ½ teaspoon of the salt. Sauté until just cooked through, about 1½ minutes per side. Remove from the heat and allow to cool to room temperature.

Bring a medium pot of salted water to a boil and blanch the radishes for about 2 minutes. Drain, and chill them quickly in a bowl of ice water. Strain out the radishes and slice them finely.

Slice the cucumbers equally finely. Mince the onion and lemon balm leaving a few leaves whole for garnish if you like, and place the cucumbers, radishes, onion, and lemon balm in a medium salad bowl. Add the crème fraîche, the remaining ¾ teaspoon of salt, and pepper, and mix well, adding more salt, if desired.

To make the plating sauce, if using: Place the Muscat, shrimp shells, orange zest and juice, piment d'Espelette, and salt in a medium saucepan over high heat and simmer until the liquid is thick enough to coat the back of a spoon. Strain and reserve this sauce before the shells absorb it.

When serving, top the cucumbers and radishes with the shrimp, and either drizzle the sauce on the shrimp or serve beside the salad on the plate.

BRAISED QUAILS *with* BRUSSELS SPROUTS & HORSERADISH

MARMITE DE CAILLES, DE CHOUX DE BRUXELLES ET DE RAIFORT

One evening Pauline got to telling the story of how her potato salad for 100 guests was the bomb because of the secret ingredient: horseradish. The next day I wanted to make a stew with rabbit and mustard, but my wife vetoed the rabbit and I was out of mustard. The Polish side of our pantry always has some prepared horseradish on hand, and everything else fell into place once I settled on quails. While I would normally keep the skin on any poultry while roasting for flavor and appearance, I often prefer to remove it when stewing as it makes unappealing rubbery bits floating around and leaves an extra pool of fat on top of the sauce.

Serves 4

1 leek, trimmed

1 stalk celery

2 tablespoons (28 g) unsalted butter

4 quails, skin removed

1 teaspoon sea salt, plus more for seasoning

10 ounces (280 g) yellow wax beans, trimmed

11 ounces (310 g) Brussels sprouts, trimmed and halved

1 tablespoon brown rice flour

¾ cup (175 ml) water

¾ cup (175 ml) heavy whipping cream

1 teaspoon fresh horseradish or Dijon mustard

⅓ cup (15 g) chopped fresh dill

½ teaspoon freshly ground black pepper

Large-dice the leek, wash well in a colander, and drain. Medium-dice the celery. Melt the butter over medium heat in a large stewing pot or sauté pan. Add the whole quails and brown on all sides. Stir in the leek, celery, and salt, and cook, covered, for about 10 minutes, stirring occasionally.

Meanwhile, bring a large pot of salted water to a boil and blanch the beans until just tender, about 5 minutes. Drain, then plunge into a bowl of cold water for 30 seconds; drain and set aside. Repeat this step with the Brussels sprouts, which should remain bright green. Drain off the cold water as soon as the Brussels sprouts have cooled.

Whisk the flour into the quail mixture, add the water, and bring to a simmer. Simmer for 5 minutes. Add the cream, flip the quails over, cover, and simmer gently for another 25 minutes, adding more water as necessary if the pot becomes dry. Finally, add the horseradish, dill, beans, Brussels sprouts, and more salt, if desired. Cook all together for about 10 minutes, stirring well and continuing to add water, if necessary.

To make the dainty ladies at your dinner party happy, you might not want to serve them whole quails, which are a little irritating to have to take a fork and knife to. Rather, allow the quails to cool to the touch in the kitchen well before serving and then pull off the legs from the carcass. With a paring knife and your fingertips, remove the breast meat from the carcass. Put the legs and breasts back in the stew to reheat along with the black pepper, while discarding the carcasses.

SEA BASS STEWED *with* SHRIMP, SCALLOPS & CREAM

RAGOÛT CRÉMEUX DE BAR SAUVAGE, DE CREVETTES, ET DE NOIX DE ST-JACQUES

A lot of substitution is possible for fish and seafood stews, but the ideal is fresh, firm fish. Flatfish like sole are too delicate for a stew, and will break apart unless you roll up the fillets and stick them with a toothpick. Defrosted frozen fish unfortunately has the tendency to break up or get mushy when cooked, with some exceptions like tuna or swordfish. In France we have a huge abundance of fresh scallops, when in season, so I'm never tempted by frozen ones. On the other hand, the "fresh" shrimp you might find at the fishmonger is almost always thawed previously frozen shrimp, so I prefer to buy it frozen for optimum freshness. If you live in inland areas and only have access to frozen fish and seafood and are happy with the quality, continue with what works for you.

Of course, the actual cooking times will depend on the size of seafood and diced fish you have in front of you, so do some reflecting before you start throwing stuff in the pot!

Serves 4 to 6

6 to 10 fingerling potatoes

1 teaspoon sea salt, plus more as needed

14 ounces (400 g) sea bass fillet

7 ounces (200 g) shell-on shrimp, fresh or frozen and thawed

10 ounces (280 g) fresh scallops

2 cups (.5 l) fresh mussels in their shells

2 tablespoons (28 g) unsalted butter, divided

1 bay leaf

2 cups (475 ml) water

1 yellow or white onion

1 stalk celery

1½ cups (355 ml) dry white wine

½ cup (120 ml) heavy whipping cream

4 sprigs fresh tarragon, leaves chopped

Bring the potatoes to a boil in salted water and cook until just tender, about 20 minutes. Drain, peel if you like (though I wouldn't), allow to cool, then medium-dice and set aside.

Prepare the fish and seafood: Remove the bones from the fish, if there are any, then large-dice. Peel and devein the shrimp, reserving the shells. Wash and trim the scallops and wash and debeard the mussels, discarding any that gape open and don't close when tapped.

Make a small stock with the shrimp shells: Heat a small pot over medium heat and melt 1 tablespoon of the butter. Add the shells, stir, and brown for 3 to 4 minutes, then add the bay leaf and cover with the 2 cups of water. Boil until reduced to ½ cup, then strain and reserve the liquid.

Heat a large stewing pot and melt the remaining tablespoon of butter over medium heat. Medium-dice the onion and the celery. Just after the butter stops foaming, add the vegetables to the pot and cook, covered, for 7 minutes without browning. Add the wine and shrimp stock, and bring to a boil, uncovered, over high heat for 5 minutes. Add the cream and bring to a simmer. Add the mussels and cook, covered, for 1 minute to build up steam. Then lower the heat to low and add the fish chunks. After 1 minute, add the scallops. Wait another minute before adding the shrimp, tarragon, and diced cooked potato. Season to taste while heating, covered, over low heat. Discard the mussels that don't open and check the largest pieces of fish for doneness before serving.

LES MARCHÉS FRANÇAIS

BEEF, ARTICHOKE & GREEN LENTIL STEW

DAUBE À LA PROVENÇAL AUX ARTICHAUTS ET AUX LENTILLES VERTES

A classic daube provençal isn't much more than a boeuf bourguignon with the addition of some olives. Why not intensify your memories of Provence with the addition of some rosemary and artichokes? I also chose to make the stew less meat-heavy by using lentils, although they're more commonly paired with lamb in French cooking. I'm not a vegetarian, but most of us eat much more meat than necessary, and all that animal rearing is such a downer for the planet. So, next time you're feeling the need for a meat stew, also think of at least five vegetables to add.

Serves 4 to 6

2 pounds (900 g) beef shank meat

¼ cup (60 ml) olive oil, divided

1 shank bone

2 shallots

2 cloves garlic

1 tablespoon brown rice flour, or your preferred thickening flour

1 cup (235 ml) dry red wine

1 teaspoon sea salt, plus more for seasoning

Pinch of dried hot chile pepper

2 large globe artichokes

1 stalk celery

1 large sprig rosemary

1 cup (170 g) dried green lentils

½ cup (100 g) pitted and halved black olives

½ bunch fresh parsley

1 teaspoon freshly ground black pepper

Cut the beef into roughly 2-inch (5 cm) pieces. Heat a wide sauté pan over medium-high heat and add 2 tablespoons (30 ml) of the oil, the beef, and the shank bone. Brown on all sides. Do this in batches, if necessary, rather than crowding all the meat together, which will have it boiling rather than browning. Mince the shallots and garlic and cook with the meat for 2 to 3 minutes without browning. Dissolve the flour into this mixture and then add the wine to deglaze the pan. If you're browning the meat in two batches, add the wine after the second batch. Simmer the wine for about 5 minutes and transfer all the meat, the shank bone, and the wine into a bigger braising pot, if necessary. It has to be big enough to eventually hold the remaining ingredients (approximately 4 quarts/3.8 liters).

Add the salt, chile pepper, and enough cold water to just cover all the beef and the bone. Simmer for about 3 hours, or until tender, adding water as necessary to keep the pan from going dry.

Meanwhile, trim the artichokes with a chef's knife and cut off the green leaves. Scoop and scrape out the fuzzy choke and discard. Medium-dice the artichoke hearts and celery. Heat a saucepan or another sauté pan, add the remaining 2 tablespoons (30 ml) of oil, and cook the artichoke hearts, celery, and rosemary for about 5 minutes, covered. Then add the lentils and enough water to fully cover. Simmer covered until tender but firm, about 20 minutes, adding more water if necessary.

Finally, add the lentil mixture to the beef, along with the olives, parsley, and black pepper. Cook together over low heat for another 15 minutes before serving, adding more salt, if desired. As with most stews, the final consistency of the liquid should be that of a thickened sauce that coats the back of a spoon.

GRATIN OF SALMON & WHITE ASPARAGUS

FILETS DE SAUMON EN GRATIN AUX ASPERGES BLANCHES

This recipe calls for the large white asparagus that's about as wide as the handle of a hammer or chef's knife. After peeling and braising until tender, it will still have a nice firm consistency, whereas the scrawny little ones often just become a fibrous mush. If you can't get fat white asparagus, it would be better to go with green, but if you want to cook them together with the salmon, it would still be better that they be as large as possible. Many people think that making a gratin means topping with cheese and/or bread crumbs, but it's not the case. The essence of a gratin is that the dish be placed under the hot broiler for at least long enough for a crispy, brown crust to be formed. With many vegetables or fish it's better to keep the gratin relatively light and pure, which is possible even with some heavy cream. Save the heavy gratin for your next macaroni and cheese.

Serves 6

⅓ leek, trimmed

1 teaspoon sea salt

1 bay leaf

2 sprigs fresh thyme

2 tablespoons (12 g) tender, minced celery leaves, or ½ teaspoon celery seeds

1 cup (235 ml) heavy whipping cream

½ cup (120 ml) water

12 large white asparagus, about the thickness of a chef's knife handle

6 (5-ounce/140 g) portions salmon fillet, or one whole fillet (about 2 pounds/900 grams)

Mince the leek and rinse it well in a colander. Place it in a medium pot along with the salt and all of the herbs and liquids and bring to a simmer. Continue to simmer for about 5 minutes, or until the leeks are just tender. Remove from the heat and set aside.

Preheat the oven on the broiler setting to 400°F (200°C). Trim and peel the white asparagus: the larger the better, in terms of final texture. You need to normally peel two layers off the asparagus, or until you have a pearly ivory surface with no trace of shiny yellow.

Place the salmon fillets in a large baking pan, with a finger's width of space between them. Lay the asparagus beside the fish in a single layer and pour the liquid and leeks from the pot over the asparagus and salmon. Immediately place the pan just above the middle of the oven. Broil the asparagus and salmon for about 10 minutes, or until the asparagus has browned nicely and the salmon is medium-well done in the center. You will need to rotate the asparagus halfway through the cooking if you see the top of the asparagus above the level of the cream at the beginning of cooking. The asparagus should be fully tender when you pierce it with a fork. By the end of cooking, the cream should have reduced and thickened, so don't expect the asparagus to be fully covered in cream at the end of cooking.

COD & SPINACH STEAMED ON SMOKED TEA LEAVES

DOS DE CABILLAUD EN PAPILLOTE AROMATISÉ AU THÉ FUMÉ

Steaming fish in parchment paper packages is a little tricky when it comes to perfect cooking times, since you can't see what's happening to your hidden piece of fish. Before serving your boss completely raw fish for his birthday dinner, practice on your family members a couple of times. The more dramatic presentation allows your guests to open the baked packages on their plate at the table so their nostrils are tickled with the escaping aromas. A more practical and time-saving method is to cook the fish all together rather than in individual packages. If you have a tagine dish or a well-sealing ovenproof dish or pan, this can work also, as long as it's large enough to hold all the fish in a single layer, separating the fish from the bed of tea leaves by parchment paper.

The taste of smoked black tea is very evocative for me of my first trip to the Atlantic coast, not in France but in Canada. While I'm not that crazy about a cup of plain black tea, I find smoked black tea irresistible in its balance of complexity in aroma and delicacy in taste.

Home-smoking may be a growing trend with restaurants or home chefs in North America, but it's not easy to imagine in Paris, where almost everyone lives in apartments. If you want to add some smoked flavor to your menu, another option is to get inventive with such condiments as smoked salt or smoked dried peppers.

Serves 6

2 pounds (900 g) skin-on fresh cod, halibut, or sea bass

Sea salt

2 medium-size leeks

2 tablespoons (28 g) unsalted butter

5 ounces (140 g) fresh spinach

6 tablespoons (18 g) smoked tea leaves, such as Lapsang Souchong

¾ cup (175 ml) heavy whipping cream

½ cup (120 ml) water

1 sprig fresh thyme

1 bay leaf

⅛ teaspoon white wine vinegar

⅛ cup (6 g) minced fresh chives

½ teaspoon crushed pink peppercorns

Trim the fish into 5-ounce (140 g) portions, while leaving the skin on if possible. The skin helps hold the fish together while cooking and serving, and helps flavor the fish while cooking. Salt each piece of fish very lightly with the few pinches of salt.

Trim the leeks, cut them in half lengthwise and slice them finely, then rinse and drain well in a colander. Melt the butter in a medium pot and add the leeks. Cover and cook gently over medium heat for about 5 minutes. Remove the stems from the spinach, if necessary. Wash and spin dry like salad greens, if it's not prewashed. Add to the leeks along with ½ teaspoon of sea salt and cook down, covered, for another 5 minutes. Remove from the heat.

Cut 6 squares as large as possible from a standard-size roll of parchment or waxed paper. Fold each in half and then cut out as large a heart shape as possible from each square, or if you have large, sharp scissors, try cutting a few at a time. To protect your fish from direct contact with the tea leaves, cut 6 rectangles of parchment paper roughly the size and shape of your pieces of fish.

Preheat the oven to 400°F (200°C). Place a scant tablespoon of tea leaves in the approximate shape of your fish pieces just to one side of the fold in each heart-shaped paper. Place your rectangle of paper over the tea and lay the fish, skin-side down, on the paper. Season each piece of fish with a pinch of salt. Top the fish with about one sixth of the leek mixture. To seal the package, start by folding up and pinching closed about 1 inch (2.5 cm) of paper from the top center of the heart. Continue folding over 1 inch at a time with a slight overlapping angle as you work your way down to the bottom tip of the heart. Tuck the final bit of paper under the fish package to complete the seal, and lay in a baking dish large enough to allow for space between each fish package.

Repeat the procedure for each piece of fish and place in the lower half of your oven to bake for 15 to 20 minutes, depending on the thickness of your fish.

While the fish is baking, combine the cream, water, thyme sprig, and bay leaf in a wide saucepan and simmer until thick enough to coat the back of a spoon. Remove from the heat and discard the bay leaf and thyme stems. Add ⅛ teaspoon of sea salt and the vinegar and chives; whisk until smooth. Serve separately at the table in a sauce container, topping with the pink peppercorns. Open packets at the table carefully, to allow the steam to escape.

RHUBARB-GLAZED PORK STUFFED *with* RED ONION CONFIT

PORC LAQUÉ À LA RHUBARBE, FARCI AUX OIGNONS DOUX

You can omit the cornmeal if you want to make the onion compote for other purposes than stuffing some meat, but here it's been added just as a thickener to help keep the onions from sneaking out while the meat is roasting. You can also add a little of your favorite spices, such as cinnamon or cloves, to the onions while they're cooking. The rhubarb glaze can also work with a veal roast and poultry breasts.

Serves 6

RED ONION COMPOTE:

10 small or 3 medium-size red onions

1 tablespoon olive oil

1 bay leaf

½ teaspoon sea salt

¼ teaspoon coarsely ground black pepper

4 tablespoons (60 ml) honey

1 tablespoon sherry vinegar or red wine vinegar

1 tablespoon fine cornmeal

RHUBARB-GLAZED TENDERLOIN:

3 stalks rhubarb (about 200 g)

2 shallots

2 kumquats (optional)

6 tablespoons (90 ml) honey or brown rice syrup

Pinch of fresh thyme

1 tablespoon brown rice flour

2 pounds (900 g) pork tenderloin

Slice away the root and tip of each onion and halve them lengthwise. Slice finely. Set a medium pot over medium heat. Place the oil and then the onions, bay leaf, salt, and pepper in the pot. Cook, covered, for about 25 minutes, stirring and scraping the bottom of the pot every 5 minutes to avoid burning. Then add the honey and vinegar and continue to cook until all the water has evaporated and the onions begin to caramelize lightly. Stir in the cornmeal and cook, stirring, for 2 minutes. Remove from the heat and allow to cool in a bowl.

Medium-dice the rhubarb and place in the bottom of a large sauté pan. Heat, covered, over low heat while mincing the shallots and kumquats, if using. As soon as some liquid appears in the bottom of the pan, add the shallots, kumquats, honey, and thyme. Cook, covered, until the shallots begin to soften, about 5 minutes. Then stir in the flour until dissolved and, using the back of your spoon to crush the rhubarb pieces, continue to cook over medium heat for another 5 minutes, or until the mixture is sticky and thick. Remove from the heat and allow to cool to room temperature.

Preheat the oven to 320°F (160°C).

To create a cavity in the pork for stuffing, insert a sharpening steel into the middle of the end and push it lengthwise through to the other end. (The steel pushes easily through the meat, and it's not difficult to keep it centered if you advance with caution.) Alternatively, preslice the tenderloin into individual portions, and use a robust paring knife to cut a hole in the pork from each end. Be sure to "reassemble" the tenderloin before cooking. Butting the pieces back against each other will help keep the onion compote from leaking out.

To stuff this cavity with the onion compote, either use a piping bag with a large, round tip or spoon it in 1 tablespoon at a time, while pushing the compote deeper inside with the back of the spoon. It can be easier to hold the tenderloin vertically so that gravity can play its role.

Lay the pork in a baking dish or roasting pan, and cover evenly with the rhubarb glaze. Place just above the middle rack of the oven and roast until a meat thermometer reads 150°F (65°C) for medium-well or a little pink in middle, and until the rhubarb mix begins to caramelize.

GREEN LENTIL & TOULOUSE SAUSAGE STEW

MARMITE DE LENTILLES VERTES ET SAUCISSE DE TOULOUSE

France's most famous lentils are from Puy, in the southern volcanic region, but you can use any green lentils as long as they keep a little al dente mouthfeel and don't cook down into a mush. Optionally, mince the spinach leaves for a more compact salad. Or separate some of them from the mixture to serve as a bed for the lentil and sausage mixture. This dish can either be a warm salad or a hot side dish. Toulouse sausages are easy to find in Parisian butcher shops, but you can use any good-quality raw sausage, preferably organic if you're not sure of its origins.

Serves 4 to 6

1 cup (180 g) dried green lentils

2 cups (475 ml) water or stock

1 teaspoon sea salt, plus more for seasoning

¼ cup (60 ml) olive oil, divided

5 ounces (140 g) raw Toulouse sausage

2 green onions

2 tablespoons (8 g) minced fresh dill

4 ounces (115 g) fresh spinach

½ teaspoon freshly ground black pepper

2 cloves garlic

Minced chives, for garnish

Cook the lentils, covered, in a medium pot with the water and salt, according to the length of time on your package instructions, Meanwhile, medium-dice the sausage. Heat a large sauté pan over medium heat, add 3 tablespoons (45 ml) of the oil with the sausage and lightly brown for 5 minutes. Mince the green onions and cook with the sausage 1 minute without browning. Thinly slice the spinach, stirring into the sausage with the dill and cooking down the spinach until wilted. Then mix in the cooked lentils to heat through with the black pepper, adding more salt if desired. Finely slice the garlic. Heat a small sauté pan over medium heat and add the remaining olive oil. Gently cook the garlic for about 1 minute, or until it just begins to lightly brown. Serve the lentils and garnish with a few slices of sautéed garlic and a sprinkle of chives.

BLACK LENTILS SIMMERED with CHARD AND SMOKED BACON

LENTILLES BELUGA MIJOTÉES AUX BLETTES ET À LA POITRINE FUMÉE

In French these black lentils are called Beluga for their resemblance to caviar. Such an allusion is also an encouragement to try to cook them with classy ingredients and to try to give some elegance to the final look and taste. We rounded up some enticing and colorful varieties of Swiss chard for this. To add another dimension to the presentation, reserve a little of the sautéed vegetables and bacon to sprinkle on top after plating. If you prefer to keep this a vegetarian dish, you can replace the bacon with smoked tofu and the chicken stock with water.

Serves 4 to 6

6 to 8 fingerling potatoes

7 ounces (200 g) smoked bacon

1 tablespoon olive oil

1 yellow or white onion

3 carrots

2 cloves garlic

4 large leaves Swiss chard

1 cup (170 g) Beluga lentils

1 bay leaf

1 sprig fresh thyme

1 teaspoon sea salt, plus more for seasoning

1 teaspoon freshly ground black pepper

2 cups (475 ml) chicken stock or water

Scrub the potatoes, cover with salted cold water in a small pot and simmer for 15 to 20 minutes, or until tender when pierced with a paring knife. Drain, medium-dice once cool to the touch, and set aside.

Heat a saucepan over medium heat. Dice the bacon and add with the oil to the pot. Brown the bacon lightly for 5 minutes. Meanwhile, small-dice the onion and carrots. Add to the pot, stir, and continue to cook, covered, for 5 minutes. Mince the garlic, add, and cook for another 5 minutes. Separate the leaves and stems of the chard. Small-dice the stems and add to the pot along with the lentils, bay leaf, thyme, salt, pepper, and or stock.

Simmer, covered, until the lentils are tender, about 20 minutes, adding more stock or water if the pot is getting dry. Thinly slice the chard leaves and stir in, cooking for another 5 minutes and adding more salt if desired. Add the diced potato just to heat through.

WILD RICE SALAD *with* DRIED ORCHARD FRUITS & CHARD

SALADE DE RIZ SAUVAGE, DE FRUITS SECS DU VERGER ET DE FEUILLES DE BLETTE

If you can't find Swiss chard, substitute any cooking greens that are in season. Where I'm from in Canada, wild rice is one of the emblematic foods. It's readily available in French supermarkets and organic stores, and I've tried to give it a French touch by adding local ingredients. Once again, this could be a served as a warm salad or as a hot side dish. Top with some toasted walnuts or hazelnuts, if you like.

Serves 4 to 6

4 ounces (115 g) uncooked wild rice

1 teaspoon sea salt, plus more for salting water

2½ cups (590 ml) water

2 ounces (55 g) dried pears

2 stalks celery

1 ounce (28 g) dried Mirabelle plums

2 ounces (55 g) dried peaches

1 bunch Swiss chard, any bad bits discarded and stems trimmed

½ cup (120 ml) walnut oil

2 tablespoons (30 ml) chardonnay vinegar

Honey (optional)

In a small pot over medium heat, combine the wild rice and water, and salt generously. Simmer, covered, for about 1 hour. When tender and fluffed and all the water is absorbed, remove from the heat and allow to cool quickly in a large salad bowl.

Meanwhile, reconstitute the dried fruits in hot water only if necessary, if they have a tough and leathery texture. Cut them all into a medium dice. Mince the celery and add to the cooled rice along with all the fruit.

Bring a large pot of water to a boil. Add the chard leaves, and after the water returns to a boil, blanch the chard for 1 minute. Meanwhile, prepare a large bowl of ice water. Remove the chard from the boiling water, stir around in the ice water for 30 seconds, then drain again and squeeze out the extra water. Pile the leaves together and mince (chiffonade) before adding to the rice mixture.

In a small bowl, whisk together the oil, vinegar, and the 1 teaspoon salt and then mix well with the rice. Add a little spoonful of honey, if desired.

ARTICHOKE HEARTS STUFFED *with* MORELS AND WHITE ASPARAGUS

FONDS D'ARTICHAUTS AUX MORILLES ET AUX ASPERGES BLANCHES

I think may soon change my last name to "Artichaut" as I find myself cooking with artichokes so often around Paris. They're too much work for me to bother with at home, but they're always a hit at dinner parties for my clients. Because they are grown both in the north of France and in the south, there's an endless variety of recipes where you can incorporate their rather neutral flavor. Morels are my favorite mushroom when it comes time to really go high class. The large dried ones are preferable for ease of cleaning, and luckily a little goes a long way as their price tag is prohibitive. You can serve these artichokes on a bed of nice spinach leaves tossed with olive oil and salt, if you like, and garnish with a basil spring and an edible flower, if you have them available.

Serves 6

Grated zest and juice of 1 lemon

1 onion of any kind, trimmed

1 clove garlic

1 bay leaf

2 sprigs fresh thyme

2 teaspoons sea salt

8 to 10 peppercorns

6 large artichokes, globe or Camus

FILLING:

1 ounce (28 g) dried morels (see note)

6 large or 12 thin white asparagus spears, peeled

2 tablespoons (28 g) unsalted butter

1 large leek (substitute white onion), minced and rinsed well

½ teaspoon sea salt

¼ teaspoon freshly ground black pepper

½ bunch fresh chives

Fill a large pot about one third of the way up with water and add the lemon juice and zest as well as the onion, garlic, bay leaf, thyme, salt, and peppercorns.

Either cut off the entire thick stem at the base of each artichoke, or ideally, break it off after facilitating the break with a knife incision in the stem at the same point. Using the edge of the countertop, hold the artichoke firmly on its side and break off the stem. This removes most of the thick fibers that simply slicing through leaves behind. Holding an artichoke firmly on a cutting board, trim the artichoke with a sharp chef's knife to eventually obtain only the tender yellow heart. This can take 5 minutes when you're new at it, so be patient. Always start from the base and rotate, trimming down cautiously so as to keep the round shape and not waste any of the precious heart. Holding the heart in the palm of your hand, scoop and scrape out the fuzzy choke with a firm teaspoon. Place the heart in the water and repeat for each artichoke.

Bring the artichoke hearts to a simmer over medium heat and cook, uncovered, for about 30 minutes, or until firm to the touch but easily pierced with a paring knife. As long as they haven't already overcooked, remove the pot from the heat and allow the artichoke hearts to cool in the cooking liquid. This artichoke cooking can be done a day ahead of time.

To make the filling: Place the dried morels in a closeable container, cover them with cold water, and shake them vigorously to remove any sand. Drain and repeat twice, discarding the water. Then pour just enough cold water over them to cover, and allow about 30 minutes for them to get tender. Much of the sand or grit will have sunk to the bottom, so without mixing that back into the mushrooms, carefully lift them out of the water and place in a bowl. Pour their soaking liquid through a coffee filter and reserve it. One last time, cover the morels with cold water and shake well before draining.

Halve all the morels to double-check for any serious grit (see note). Remember that it's impossible to remove all the possible bits of earth and forest from wild mushrooms.

Preheat the oven to 350°F (175°C).

Cut all the asparagus into medium dice, halving the large ones lengthwise first. Heat a wide sauté pan over medium heat and melt the butter. Add the asparagus, leek, and morels. Cover and cook for 5 minutes, to soften, and then add the cream, salt, and pepper. Cover and simmer for another 5 minutes, adding enough of the reserved morel soaking liquid to keep it from getting too thick, and then mince and stir in the chives off the heat.

Fill the cooked artichoke hearts with this mixture and place them in a baking dish. Bake on the middle rack of the oven for about 15 minutes, before serving with some arugula or spinach greens.

Note: Sometimes there are just one or two muddy morels in the batch that ruin it for them all, so before I cut each one in half lengthwise after reconstituting, I rub them a bit on my cutting board to see whether extra washing is necessary. The goal, of course, is to not wash away all their flavor and aroma before the cooking even begins.

CHOCOLATE LAVA CAKES FILLED *with* RASPBERRY & WHITE CHOCOLATE

MI-CUITS AU CHOCOLAT NOIR, CŒURS DE FRAMBOISE ET CHOCOLAT BLANC

This is one of the many variations of the original molten-center chocolate cakes invented by the French three-star chef Michel Bras in 1980. Not everything in France goes back to Louis XIV! The most classic version of the cake is pure dark chocolate, and a cube of frozen ganache is placed into the center of the batter and stays runny after the surrounding cake batter has become solid. Optionally, serve with a raspberry coulis and vanilla ice cream.

Makes 6

8 ounces (225 g) dark chocolate (60% to 70% cacao)

½ cup (115 g) unsalted butter, plus 4 tablespoons (55 g), for ramekins

5 large eggs

4 ounces (115 g) dark brown sugar, plus more for dusting

7 tablespoons (64 g) chestnut flour or brown rice flour

12 raspberries

¼ cup (60 ml) heavy whipping cream

3 ounces (85 g) white chocolate, broken into 12 squares

Fresh red currants or raspberries, for garnish

Confectioners' sugar, for dusting

Preheat the oven to 450°F (230°C). Melt the dark chocolate and ½ cup (110 g) of butter together in a stainless-steel bowl placed over a pot of simmering water until just melted, not touching the water. Remove from the heat and allow to cool enough to touch the bottom of the bowl without burning your fingers.

In a separate large bowl, beat the eggs and sugar with an electric mixer for about 3 minutes, to add some air to the eggs. Pour the warm chocolate mixture into the eggs and stir until homogenous. Sift in the flour and mix gently until all the flour is incorporated. Butter 6 small individual ramekins with the remaining 4 tablespoons (55 g) of butter and dust with sugar. Silicone or aluminum ramekins work the best for unmolding and plating after, which is quite difficult in the case of porcelain ramekins.

Fill the ramekins halfway with the batter. Push 2 raspberries into the center of each, with their holes facing up. Drizzle the cream into the holes until they are full and top each with 2 squares of white chocolate pressed together. Cover with the remaining batter to just under the upper edge of each ramekin.

Bake on the bottom rack of the oven for 6 to 7 minutes, or until the sides have fully risen but the centers remain concave. Remove from the oven and allow to cool for 1 minute before inverting onto dessert plates. If necessary, first free the sides with paring knife before inverting. If you have fully cooled these cakes before serving, the center will not be runny, but a few seconds in the microwave just before serving can help. Keep practicing until you've got the timing down with your oven. Garnish with red currants and dust with confectioners' sugar.

GRATIN OF BERRIES & GRAND MARNIER SABAYON

GRATIN DE FRUITS ROUGES ET SABAYON AU GRAND MARNIER

This is a great go-to dessert when you have some fresh fruit around and limited time to cook for some last-minute guests. Use only whole, uncut berries or this dessert will turn into berry soup. When it's not berry season, you could use fresh peaches, apricots, or figs. It works equally well with many tropical fruits, such as mango, pineapple, and banana, in winter, replacing the Grand Marnier with rum.

Serves 6

18 to 20 ounces (510 to 570 g) fresh whole berries of your choice

6 large egg yolks

½ cup (120 ml) honey

2 tablespoons (30 ml) dry white wine

2 tablespoons (30 ml) water

2 tablespoons (30 ml) Grand Marnier or other orange liqueur

6 tablespoons dark brown sugar, divided

Wash and trim the berries and use them to line the bottom of 6 individual gratin or crème brûlée dishes.

Place the egg yolks in a medium sauté pan. Whisk in the honey, wine, water, and Grand Marnier and place over low heat. Whisk constantly until the eggs are light, creamy, and thickened into a custard, but before any egg begins to coagulate into solid bits, 5 to 7 minutes. Initially steam will begin to rise from the mixture. When the eggs are cooked enough, you will see traces of the pan bottom with each whisking motion. Immediately remove from the heat if you ever see traces of solid egg. An instant-read thermometer will read 165°F (74°C) if you choose to use one.

Turn on the oven to its maximum broiler setting and make sure there's an oven rack just under the broiler. The goal is not to preheat the whole oven, as these desserts are not for baking. The goal is just having a hot broiler to quickly caramelize the tops.

Sprinkle 1 tablespoon of the sugar over the berries in each dish and then cover each dish with equal amounts of the egg mixture. Wait until the broiler element is red hot, and then place the dishes on the top rack of the oven. Check closely to make sure they don't burn. After a minute or two you should have some light caramelization, without overcooking the eggs or fruit.

Remove those desserts that are perfectly browned and continue to brown the others, if necessary. Serve warm.

STRAWBERRY & CHAMPAGNE SOUP *with* DARK CHOCOLATE MOUSSE

SOUPE AUX FRAISES ET AU CHAMPAGNE ROSÉ ET SA MOUSSE AU CHOCOLAT NOIR

It's fun to have another excuse to open Champagne besides birthday parties and wedding anniversaries! You will feel delectably decadent emptying a bottle of bubbles into the soup. In France there are some good-quality sparkling wines that would do just as well as Champagne in this dessert: look for prosecco, cava, or even American domestic sparkling wines. Whether you use Champagne or sparkling wine depends on if your dinner guests are high or low maintenance. When I'm making mousse in France I use raw eggs with very little worry about salmonella, but this recipe is for all of you that would prefer to be on the safe side and have pasteurized eggs. My favorite texture and richness for mousses is for them to have both beaten cream and eggs.

Serves 6

CHOCOLATE MOUSSE:

7 ounces (200 g) dark chocolate (60% to 70% cacao)

½ cup (115 g) unsalted butter

3 large egg yolks

1 large egg

⅔ cup packed (122 g) dark brown sugar

1 cup (235 ml) very cold heavy whipping cream

STRAWBERRY AND CHAMPAGNE SOUP:

2 pounds (900 g) fresh strawberries

½ cup (120 ml) honey, or more to taste

1 vanilla bean, split and seeds scraped

1 cup (235 ml) brut pink Champagne or sparkling wine (save the rest for serving with dessert)

Square of white chocolate, for grating

To make the chocolate mousse: Melt the chocolate with the butter in a double boiler or a heatproof bowl set over a small pot of simmering water, without the bowl touching the water. Stir until melted, then remove from the heat and allow to cool to near room temperature.

Meanwhile, place the egg yolks, egg, and sugar in medium sauté pan and whisk over low heat until thickened and lightly pasteurized at 165°F (74°C). If you don't have a thermometer, there are signs to watch for: steam will be coming off the eggs, and you should see traces of the bottom of the pan while whisking, but no solid bits should be forming. Stop heating before the mixture reaches full coagulation and quickly empty out the eggs into a bowl to cool. While still warm, mix the chocolate into the eggs.

Put the cream in a large, dry, clean bowl, and whip with an electric mixer on high speed until stiff peaks form: when you lift the whisk attachment, the peaks will hold a firm shape, and the cream will wiggle a little from what clings to the whisk, but won't drip off. Fold the whipped cream into the chocolate mixture in thirds, making sure the mixture is homogenous only on the final addition of cream. Do not mix beyond this point, as you will only be collapsing the air volume from the mousse.

There are at least three presentation options: spoon it into a medium or large glass bowl and scoop out servings, divide it among individual parfait glasses, or pipe it into individual pastry circles on plates. However you do it, chill for 2 hours minimum. The general idea is to have a center of mousse with the strawberry soup around it.

To make the soup: Set aside about 18 strawberries and halve them, then puree purée the remaining strawberries, honey, and vanilla bean seeds. Add more honey if the strawberries are not very ripe. The strawberry purée should taste a little oversweet, assuming that you're adding a good-quality dry Champagne later. Chill well but try to serve this soup a little warmer than refrigerator temperature.

Before adding any Champagne, pour the strawberry purée around the plated chocolate mousse, and top each bowl with about 6 strawberry halves. If you opt for serving this dessert in one large bowl in the center of the table, pour the chilled Champagne directly from the bottle into the strawberry purée, and watch your guests' eyes light up. (Eyeball the suggested volume of Champagne, as it will look so much less dramatic if you pour Champagne from a measuring cup!) For individual desserts, I would suggest pouring a little splash of Champagne into everyone's glass, which can then be emptied into each strawberry purée. Grate white chocolate over the top and serve. Serve the remaining Champagne in glasses with dessert.

When it's impossible to find any more green or white asparagus in the markets, you know the page is turning on the spring season. Summer is my favorite season in almost every consideration and is also a favorite time to be in the markets. I get to spend far too little time every year in the South of France, so as soon as Paris gets warm and lazy, I like to pretend I'm in Provence or Languedoc. I refuse to buy butter, cream, potatoes, or any root vegetables. Although such Mediterranean vegetables as bell peppers, eggplant, tomatoes, and olives (yes, I know they're all actually fruits) are available year-round, I finally cast aside my personal restrictions on buying them out of season, and load up my shopping trolley with as much color as possible. I'm a sucker for yellow zucchini, just because they exude pure sunshine. The round green zucchini always catch my eye, too, begging me to invent a new stuffing to fill them with and bake them.

When the hot winds blow up over France from Spain and the Sahara, it's unthinkable to turn on the oven. Every day at our place, dinner is just crusty sourdough bread and a large bowl of salad based on tomatoes or melons or peaches, and always perked up with fresh herbs, such as mint and basil. There's always a bottle of chilled rosé handy, although between October and May I don't have any use for it, and all the little goat and sheep's milk cheeses from the Loire Valley and Provence are irresistible. Suddenly olives regain appeal as well—basically anything that pairs well with rosé wine and makes me feel as if I'm on vacation is all I really crave.

The tiniest fraction of Parisians lives in houses or villas, where they would have the option for lighting up the barbecue. The rest of us are lucky if our apartment has a balcony, but barbecuing is forbidden on balconies. A hint of grilling pleasure can be found in using those stovetop cast-iron grill pans, which at least leave the correct black marks on your seared tuna steak as well as a charred flavor. Anything that takes less than five minutes' cooking time—such as shrimp, red onions, or rare steaks of beef—is ideal when your kitchen is already stuffy.

One of the keys to perfecting your summer market shopping is the patience to wait for the season's fruits and vegetables to really reach their peak. The berries that appear in May can be a little sweeter in June. Melons that appear in June can be passed by without more than a passing glance; in July they'll finally be heavy with pungent ripeness. July's peaches and nectarines are usually a hard and bitter disappointment. August will offer up the best of most of the stone fruits. Trying to find the perfect fig in August? In Paris all you'll find is the thick-skinned greenish ones from Spain until September, when Solliès sends up its delicate rosy-fleshed black figs from the heart of Provence. By then, vacation and sleepy neighborhoods are a memory and all the Parisians are crowding back into their favorite markets.

Starters

Duck, Green Bean &
Toasted Almond Salad 125

Coleslaw with
Shredded Cured Savoie Ham 126

Olive-Rubbed Red Mullet
with Eggplant & Tomato 129

Portobello Mushrooms Stuffed
with Broccoli & Goat Cheese 130

Chilled Beet Soup with
Fresh Goat Cheese & Tarragon 133

Chilled Melon & Muscat Soup
with Mint Syrup 135

Cherry Tomato & Basil Clafoutis 137

Main Courses

Basque Chicken Stew
with Roasted Peppers 139

Braised Pork with Plum & Black Olive 141

Scorpion Fish Broiled in
Yellow Tomato & Saffron 142

Seared Duck Breast &
Caramelized Fennel 144

Turkey Breast with
Kale, Pecans & Garlic 146

Roast Quails with Red Currant Glaze
& Green Pea Purée 148

Lunches and Side Dishes

Corn Pasta Salad with Avocado,
Lime & Sun-Dried Tomato 152

Golden Ratatouille with
Chickpeas & Saffron 155

White Coco Beans Stewed with
Corn & Purple Potatoes 156

Fresh Paimpol Bean Stew with
Golden Chanterelles 159

Baby Peppers Stuffed with
Chorizo, Capers & Anchovies 160

Stuffed Zucchini with Fresh Sheep's
Milk Cheese & Currants 162

Desserts

Peach & Rice Pudding Gratin 164

Cherry, Almond &
Tonka Bean Cakes 167

Crêpes with Stewed Apricots,
Vanilla & Honey 168

LES MARCHÉS FRANÇAIS

DUCK, GREEN BEAN & ROASTED ALMOND SALAD

SALADE DE MAGRET DE CANARD, DE HARICOTS VERTS ET D'AMANDES GRILLÉES

My wife proposed the base of this salad and wanted credit for it, but I think the idea of combining these ingredients goes back a few generations before we came along! In some classic brasseries, green beans are served as a starter vegetable salad or side dish, but they are usually just a completely uninspired plate of green beans and vinaigrette. Anyone can do better than that. Add duck breast for the ultimate green bean salad. An alternative to the stovetop cooking suggested below is to pop the duck breast into a low oven (250°F/120°C) and roast for about 15 minutes after following the searing procedure. The breast will still be pink and moist but won't have any red rareness in the center.

Serves 4 to 6

1 teaspoon sea salt, divided, plus more for salting water and seasoning

14 ounces (400 g) trimmed green beans

½ clove garlic

1 large duck breast

1 teaspoon piment d'Espelette, or your favorite ground dried chile pepper

2 oranges

6 tablespoons (90 ml) hazelnut oil

2 tablespoons (30 ml) white wine vinegar or sherry vinegar

1 tablespoon honey

1 shallot, minced

½ cup (50 g) sliced or chopped almonds, toasted

Bring a medium pot of salted water to a boil and blanch the beans for 4 to 6 minutes, depending on size. Drain and cool quickly in a bowl of ice water. Remove from the ice water and drain well. Smash and mince the garlic clove and add along with ½ teaspoon of the salt to the beans. Transfer the bean mixture to a large salad bowl.

Trim the duck breast, score the skin, and sear, skin-side down, over medium-high heat for 7 to 10 minutes, or until browned and crispy. Turn the breast and sear the reverse side, then lower the heat and continue to cook another 10 minutes, or until semifirm to the touch and pink in the center. Toss it with the piment d'Espelette and allow it to cool to room temperature before thinly slicing. After slicing, toss the duck with the remaining ½ teaspoon of salt and add to the beans.

Cleanly cut the peel off the oranges without leaving any pith, and use a paring knife to cut out the segments while discarding the fibrous membranes. (In France this is called making orange suprêmes. If you're not afraid of fiber, and don't mind a messier presentation, you can just dice up the peeled orange with the membrane.) Cut the segments into large dice. Whisk the oil, vinegar, and honey with the shallot, and toss with the salad, topping with the almonds just before serving. Serve with additional salt, if desired.

COLESLAW with SHREDDED CURED SAVOIE HAM

SALADE DE CHOUX À LA CHIFFONNADE DE JAMBON SEC DE SAVOIE

Every supermarket in France sells premade coleslaw, but they all use the same drab idea of flavoring with nothing more than some industrial mayonnaise. There are so many variations of lettuce salad; why can't we try to be a little adventurous when it comes to cabbage salad as well? The idea behind the addition of cured ham is to enrich the complexity of flavor as well as add the protein that allows this salad to stand on its own in a simple lunch with crusty bread.

A few different regions in France have their own traditional ham-preserving techniques. I used ham from the Savoie in the foothills of the Alps, but you can use any cured ham, such as the Italian prosciutto.

Serves 4

3 ounces (85 g) cured Savoie ham or prosciutto

9 ounces (255 g) finely shredded green cabbage (or red, if you prefer)

⅓ cup (20 g) minced fresh parsley

¾ cup (175 g) full-fat yogurt

2 tablespoons (30 ml) white wine vinegar

1 tablespoon honey or agave syrup, or more to taste

1 teaspoon sea salt, or more to taste

1 teaspoon aniseeds

Finely slice the cured ham, one slice at a time, to prevent the slices from sticking together. In a large salad bowl, mix in well with the cabbage. In a small bowl, whisk the parsley, yogurt, vinegar, honey, salt, and aniseed and toss with the cabbage mixture, adding more salt or honey, if desired. Allow to rest for 1 hour before serving, so the cabbage will become more tender.

OLIVE-RUBBED RED MULLET *with* EGGPLANT & TOMATO

ROUGET-BARBET AUX OLIVES VERTES ET SA RISTE D'AUBERGINES

This fish has a built-in side dish in the form of an eggplant and tomato stew that originates from the South of France and is about as simple and rustic as it can get. It's like they wanted to make a ratatouille but were missing its bell peppers and zucchini. Since it is also not as vibrant in color as ratatouille, you may want to jazz it up with multicolored tomatoes and maybe some parsley. Red mullet doesn't have a cool name in English. You can replace it with the much fancier-sounding "red snapper," but since it is a much larger fish, it would be better to cut each fillet down into about six finger-size portions if you are trying to make this dish as a pretty appetizer. If you like, serve with arugula or spinach greens.

Serves 6

2 medium-size eggplants

1 tablespoon plus ½ teaspoon sea salt, plus more as needed

7 tablespoons (100 ml) olive oil, diveded, plus more as needed

1 large onion, medium-diced

1 bay leaf

2 sprigs fresh thyme

3 cloves garlic, divided

2 large tomatoes

24 green olives

Juice of ½ lemon

¼ cup (60 ml) olive oil, plus more for brushing

Pinch of freshly ground black pepper

6 red mullets, cleaned and filleted, or 2 red snapper fillets, cut into 12 pieces

Coarse sea salt, to season fish

Arugula, for serving

Cut the eggplants into large dice and toss with the tablespoon of salt in a large bowl. After 10 minutes, rinse well with cold water and drain well in a colander. This step prevents the eggplants from absorbing the oil so readily while sautéing, and removes a little bitterness.

Heat a large nonstick sauté pan over medium-high heat and add 3 tablespoons of the oil. When the oil is hot, add the eggplants. Watch for splattering because of the wet eggplants. Sauté for about 5 minutes while shaking or stirring once per minute. After the eggplants begin to brown lightly, add the onion and herbs. Cover and soften the onion over medium heat for about 7 minutes, or until translucent. Stir in 2 cloves of the garlic and cook, covered, for another 2 minutes. Large-dice the tomatoes. Increase the heat to medium-high, add the tomatoes along with the ½ teaspoon of salt, and cook, uncovered, until all the vegetables are soft and thickened. Add more salt, if desired.

Pit the olives and purée them with the remaining clove of garlic, using a small food processor or mortar and pestle. Incorporate the lemon juice, remaining 4 tablespoons of oil, a pinch of salt, and the pepper.

Turn on the broiler setting of your oven to its maximum, and place a rack on the top level of the oven. Make sure the bones have been removed from the fish, and then rub the cut side with the olive purée and place the fillets, skin-side up, in a shallow baking dish or pan. The rub should just provide a little coating that adheres, not globs that just fall off when you flip the fish over. Brush the skin with a little oil and sprinkle with coarse salt. Wait until the broiler coils are red hot and then place the fish in the oven. Broil for 4 to 5 minutes, checking to be sure the skin isn't burning.

Serve 2 fillets on each plate with about 2 rounded tablespoons of eggplant stew, using a pastry cutting form to mold the stew if you want it to look pretty on the plate, and tucking in a few pieces of arugula.

PORTOBELLO MUSHROOMS STUFFED with BROCCOLI & GOAT CHEESE

CHAMPIGNONS PORTOBELLO FARCIS AU BROCOLI ET AU CHÈVRE

These mushrooms are great as written, but of course there are ways to vary the recipe. If you don't mind adding an Italian twist, there's no reason why they couldn't work with ricotta cheese, which I would make a little richer and creamier with the addition of a big tablespoon of mascarpone. A double-crème cow's milk cheese, such as Brillat-Savarin, would also be more than satisfying. Serve these with some greens on the side, if you like.

Serves 6

½ head broccoli

½ leek or white onion

1 clove garlic

7 ounces (200 g) fresh goat cheese

½ teaspoon minced fresh rosemary

½ teaspoon sea salt

¼ teaspoon freshly ground black pepper

1 tablespoon olive oil

6 large portobello mushrooms

12 toasted walnuts (optional)

1 tablespoon sliced chives

Bring a medium pot of water to a boil. Trim the broccoli into small florets, mincing all the tender parts of the stems. Mince the leek and rinse away any grit. Mince the garlic. Parboil the broccoli, leek, and garlic for no more than 2 minutes and drain through a fine-mesh strainer so as not lose any of the vegetables. Let drain and cool for 3 to 4 minutes, and then mix it all in a large bowl with the goat cheese, rosemary, salt, and pepper.

Trim and discard the stems from the portobellos, and give them a quick rinse. Use a tablespoon or ice-cream scoop to nicely mound the broccoli mixture into the bottom of each mushroom cap. Heat the oil in a large nonstick sauté pan over low heat and add the mushrooms. Cover and cook gently for 8 to 10 minutes, to get the cheese just heated through rather than piping hot, which will cause its proteins to coagulate and result in an unpleasantly grainy texture.

Crumble the walnuts, if using, over the top with the chives and serve warm or at room temperature, with the mushroom cooking juices spooned over the top.

CHILLED BEET SOUP *with* FRESH GOAT CHEESE & TARRAGON

SOUPE FROIDE AUX BETTERAVES, AU FROMAGE DE CHÈVRE FRAIS, ET À L'ESTRAGON

In France it's rather exotic to find raw beets in the markets as there is a predominance of precooked beets available. This is true of both farmers' markets and supermarkets. You can count on the organic markets and shops to come through with the fresh beets when they're in season. If you live somewhere that doesn't sell good goat or sheep's milk cheese, you could try the easy-to-find ricotta, but you may want to add a dash more vinegar to give a little more tanginess to the soup. Feta cheese would add tanginess all on its own.

I would suggest red or yellow beets for this soup, or a mixture of both to create orange, but the cute white and pink striped ones would dull down the color too much once puréed.

Serves 6

5 small or 3 large red or yellow beets, with greens, if possible

2 shallots, minced

½ teaspoon fresh thyme

4 cups (945 ml) water

1 teaspoon sea salt, plus a pinch for the greens (optional)

5 ounces (140 g) fresh, moist goat or sheep's milk cheese

1 teaspoon cider vinegar

1 tablespoon minced fresh tarragon (from about 2 large sprigs)

Peel the beets and medium-dice, reserving any fresh and tender greens. Place in a medium pot and add the shallots, thyme, and water. Bring to a simmer over medium-high heat, cover, and continue to cook until the beets are tender, 30 to 40 minutes.

Remove from the heat and allow the pot to cool to room temperature. Add the 1 teaspoon salt, half of the cheese, and the vinegar and purée well with an immersion blender or in a food processor. Stir in three quarters of the tarragon, reserving the rest for garnish. Add more water if the soup is too thick.

If you've been able to save the fresh and tender beet greens, wash them and then blanch them for 2 minutes in boiling water. Drain and chill quickly in a bowl of ice water, and then drain again. Chop roughly and purée in an immersion blender cup, adding a drizzle of water, if necessary, to help the blender work the leaves into a thick purée. Add a pinch of salt and spoon on the top of each serving as garnish.

Crumble up the remaining goat cheese as a garnish, and top each serving with the remaining tarragon.

LES MARCHÉS FRANÇAIS

CHILLED MELON & MUSCAT SOUP *with* MINT SYRUP

SOUPE FRAÎCHE AU MELON, AU MUSCAT ET AU SIROP DE MENTHE

This soup could also be a dessert if you added a little more honey, but I prefer it as a starter, accompanied by toasted country bread brushed with olive oil and topped with your favorite shaved cured ham (we chose one from Bayonne). As with most fruit soups, the level of satisfaction with final result will depend largely on the ripeness of the fruit, so find the best, ripest melons you can lay your hands on.

Serves 4 to 6

2 large, ripe cantaloupes

3 tablespoons (65 g) honey

½ cup (120 ml) Muscat wine or sweet Porto

1 to 2 teaspoons cider vinegar

½ teaspoon sea salt

½ teaspoon coarsely ground black pepper

MINT SYRUP:

1 bunch fresh mint

2 tablespoons (30 ml) water

2 tablespoons (30 ml) honey

Cut the melons in half, remove the seeds, and use a melon baller or teaspoon measure to make balls for the soup garnish, about 5 per person. Scoop out the remaining flesh into a food processor and blend with the honey, Muscat, vinegar, salt, and pepper. Chill for at least 2 hours.

To make the mint syrup: Wash the mint and remove all the leaves from the stems. Bring the water and honey to a simmer in a small pot over high heat and then stir in the mint leaves. Remove immediately from the heat and allow to steep for 20 to 30 seconds before blending well with an immersion blender. For a less strong mint flavor, you can steep the mint leaves for 3 to 4 minutes and then strain out the leaves. In any case, immediately transfer the syrup from the hot pan to a small jar or bowl, and place in a little bowl of ice water to cool it quickly.

Serve the chilled soup with the melon balls floating on top, and a drizzle of mint syrup.

CHERRY TOMATO & BASIL CLAFOUTIS

CLAFOUTIS AUX TOMATES CERISES ET AU BASILIC

The most famous clafoutis is indeed the dessert variety with cherries, but without the sugar it lends itself to many savory variations. Keep the tomatoes whole or you will have a wet and sloppy stewed tomato–scrambled egg dish, which nobody wants! For a dinner party it's definitely cuter to serve this in individual gratin dishes. Trying to cut wedges from a large pie plate is bound to get messy, as clafoutis doesn't have a crust like a quiche to hold it all together. What's more, it will cool very rapidly once you've set a piece on an unheated plate, and ramekins will hold heat much better. I used small gratin dishes—just over five inches (14 cm)—eight to ten cherry tomatoes fit in each of these.

Serves 6

27 to 30 ounces (765 to 850 g) cherry tomatoes (50 to 60 tomatoes)

¼ cup (60 ml) olive oil

3 large eggs, at room temperature

1 large egg yolk, at room temperature

½ cup (120 ml) whole milk, at room temperature

¼ cup (38 g) brown rice flour or chestnut flour

1 teaspoon sea salt

2 tablespoons (10 g) ground pecorino or Parmesan cheese

2 tablespoons (6 g) minced fresh chives

2 tablespoons (8 g) minced fresh parsley

¼ cup (10 g) minced fresh basil

Preheat the oven to 350°F (175°C). If you're up to it, consider the option of peeling each tomato for a much smoother-textured clafoutis. To do this, you will have to make a cross-incision with a sharp paring knife into the bottom of each tomato. Place on a nonstick cookie sheet or shallow baking dish, drizzle, with oil, and roast in the middle of the oven for 10 to 15 minutes, or until the tomato skins begin to peel back. It doesn't hurt to check on the tomatoes every 4 to 5 minutes to make sure they're not overcooking into some mush. The cooking time depends on the ripeness and fragility of your tomatoes. Remove from the oven and let cool to the touch before removing and discarding the tomato skins. If you can't be bothered with peeling tomatoes, simply follow the roasting technique without the incisions or the peeling.

In a bowl, beat the eggs and egg yolk and whisk in the milk. In a separate bowl, mix the flour, salt, pecorino, chives, parsley, and basil. Beat in just enough of the egg mixture to whisk the flour mixture into a smooth paste, and then whisk in the remaining egg mixture. With this technique the batter should be naturally free of lumps, but don't overmix if you encounter just a few small lumps, or your clafoutis will come out with a rubbery texture.

Place the tomatoes either in a large gratin or flan pan, or in 6 individual gratin dishes. Add the clafoutis batter to almost completely cover the tomatoes and bake on the top rack of the oven for 15 to 25 minutes, or until a knife inserted into the center comes out clean. Try to make sure they get a little coloring and crispiness on top without overcooking, putting the clafoutis under a red-hot broiler for 30 to 60 seconds, if necessary.

LES MARCHÉS FRANÇAIS

BASQUE CHICKEN STEW *with* ROASTED PEPPERS

POULET BASQUAISE AUX POIVRONS RÔTIS

At its heart, this is a classic version of poulet basquaise, which is a popular braised dish from the Pyrenees Mountains. However, this variation adds appreciable complexity and depth to the flavor with the initial roasting of the peppers. Always pay attention to the freshness of your garlic. If you see a green shoot starting to grow from the center, be sure to remove it, to keep the garlic from overpowering the dish and sometimes upsetting your digestion. Guinea fowl would be a good substitution for chicken, if the latter is too commonplace for you.

Serves 4

4 red Anaheim peppers

4 free-range chicken legs (about 20 ounces/570 g total)

2 tablespoons (30 ml) olive oil

1 yellow or white onion

3 cloves garlic

1½ cups (355 ml) dry white wine

1 teaspoon piment d'Espelette or cayenne pepper

1 teaspoon sea salt, plus more for seasoning

4 Roma tomatoes

Leave the red peppers whole and blacken them over your gas flame, or place them directly under a broiler at its maximum setting and rotate every minute or two until all of the skin is blackened. Remove from the heat and allow to cool for 10 minutes or to the touch, then scrape off the blackened skin with the back of a paring knife and your fingertips. In no case should you rinse the pepper under water, which washes away some of the flavor, but it is usually necessary to rinse your hands repeatedly while doing this task.

Pull the skin off the chicken legs and discard. Heat a Dutch oven or large sauté pan over medium heat and add the oil. Add the chicken and brown all sides. Medium-dice the onion and add to the pot. Cover and soften the onion for 5 minutes. Mince the garlic, add, cover, and continue to cook for 5 minutes without browning. Add the wine, piment d'Espelette, and salt and simmer for about 30 minutes, turning the chicken periodically, until the sauce is slightly thickened. Core, seed, and large-dice the red peppers and add to the pot. Continue to cook while chopping the tomatoes into large dice. Add them and simmer for another 15 minutes, along with more salt, if desired. Add water if the sauce looks too thick, or simmer uncovered if the sauce is too thin. Like many stews, the resulting sauce should be just thick enough to coat the back of a spoon.

BRAISED PORK with PLUM & BLACK OLIVE

MARMITE DE PORC, DE PRUNES ET D'OLIVES

Moroccan food is extremely popular in France, and this combination of flavors is reminiscent of some of their tagines, although of course they would never use pork. You can also use poultry, veal, or lamb to replace pork in this dish. I used fresh plums as they happened to be in season, but during the rest of the year it's common to see dried prunes or other dried fruits, such as apricots, in the mixture. With a total cooking time of only 45 minutes, this is a stew that can be put together without too much advance planning.

Serves 4

14 ounces (400 g) pork loin

2 tablespoons (30 ml) olive oil

1 green bell pepper or large green Anaheim pepper

12 black olives, preferably with pits (often those sold pitted are less flavorful)

2 shallots

1 teaspoon ground coriander

½ teaspoon ground cumin

½ teaspoon ground ginger

¼ teaspoon dried hot chile pepper

1 teaspoon sea salt, plus more for seasoning

1 teaspoon freshly ground black pepper

1 preserved lemon (see page 193)

1 cup (235 ml) chicken or veal stock or water

8 purple plums

½ bunch fresh cilantro

Trim and large-dice the pork loin. Heat a large Dutch oven or wide skillet over medium-high heat, add the oil, and brown the meat lightly for 5 to 10 minutes. Large-dice the green pepper; halve the olives, pitting if necessary; and medium-dice the shallots. Along with the spices and salt, add the green pepper, olives, and shallots to the pot, lowering the heat to prevent burning the shallots. Cover and cook over low heat for another 5 minutes without browning the shallots. Large-dice the preserved lemon (discarding the seeds) and add to the pot with the stock. Bring to a simmer for 10 minutes. Meanwhile, halve, pit, and large-dice the plums. Add and simmer until the sauce has thickened, adding more salt, if desired. Roughly chop the cilantro, and add just before serving.

SCORPION FISH BROILED IN YELLOW TOMATO & SAFFRON

FILETS DE RASCASSE GRILLÉS AUX TOMATES JAUNES ET AU SAFRAN

My favorite dishes combine common, unfussy ingredients with no more than one or two more exotic ones. Here, the saffron elevates everyday ingredients to more than the sum of their parts. Showing restraint in seasoning is one hallmark of French cooking. One of the reasons for this is because drinking wine with meals is such an entrenched tradition, and a large majority of French prefer wines that are dry and mineral, which are less complementary to spicy foods.

Serves 6

3 scorpion fish or red snapper, each filleted into 2 portions

1 bulb fennel

1 red or Vidalia onion

2 tablespoons (30 ml) olive oil, plus more for brushing fish

1 clove garlic

½ teaspoon sea salt, plus more for seasoning

5 yellow tomatoes

1 or 2 pinches of saffron powder or threads

Grated zest and juice of 1 medium-size orange

Pinch of piment d'Espelette or cayenne pepper

Coarse sea salt, to season fish

Make sure you are using fish fillets with the skin still left on but cleaned of scales. The skin is usually visually appealing when cooked, plus the fat of the skin adds flavor and moisture and the skin will help your fillet hold together when serving. Remove any bones with fish pliers and score two X's into the skin to prevent too much curling of the fish during broiling.

Reserving the fennel fronds, thinly slice the bulb and stalks, if any, and the onion. Heat a large ovenproof sauté pan over low heat and add the 2 tablespoons (30 ml) oil, fennel, and onion. Cover and soften, stirring occasionally, for 10 minutes. Mince the garlic and add it along with the salt. Increase the heat to medium-high and cook for just a minute or two, to avoid browning the garlic. Large-dice the tomatoes and add along with the saffron, orange zest and juice, and piment d'Espelette. Simmer for about 10 minutes, or until the fennel is tender and the sauce has thickened. Mince the fennel fronds, if any, and stir into the sauce.

Turn on the oven broiler to HIGH and make sure there is a rack just below the broiler where you will be able to fit your sauté pan. There is no need to preheat the oven for this recipe. Place the fish, skin-side up, in the braised vegetables, brush the skin with oil, and sprinkle with coarse salt. If desired, add more salt to the vegetables.

When the broiler is red hot (2 or 3 minutes after turning it on), place the pan under the broiler and cook the fish for about 5 minutes, making sure the skin isn't too close to the heat to begin burning before the fish is done. You will see some white fish juices after coagulation and the fish should feel firm to the touch in the thickest part of the fillet.

SEARED DUCK BREAST & CARAMELIZED FENNEL

MAGRET DE CANARD AU FENOUIL CARAMÉLISÉ

I'm surprised by how many non-French people tell me that they don't like duck breast because it's dry and tough. If you insist on eating it well-done and roasted at high heat, I can guarantee you that it will indeed be dry and tough. Whether you render off the fat and aim for a thin crispy skin or prefer leaving a thick layer of fatty skin, the meat itself is quite lean; the only way to keep it moist and tender is to sear and then finish the cooking to medium doneness with gentle heat. You can choose whether to go for a slow oven or low heat on the stovetop. This recipe calls for just enough fennel to make a cute accompaniment to the duck, assuming that you're also serving another vegetable, or maybe rice. If the people you're cooking for love fennel, you can double the recipe.

Serves 4 to 6

2 small or 1 large bulb fennel

½ teaspoon sea salt

¼ cup (60 ml) aniseed liqueur, or
2 teaspoons whole aniseed

¼ cup (60 ml) olive oil

2 tablespoons (30 ml) honey

1 teaspoon white wine vinegar

3 large duck breasts (about 14 ounces/
400 g each)

2 tablespoons (30ml) water

1 teaspoon coarse sea salt

Trim off the fennel stalks, remove the green fronds, and reserve both. Quarter the small bulbs of fennel or cut the large bulb into 8 wedges. Line the fennel wedges in the bottom of wide, nonstick, ovenproof saucepan in a single layer and add the stalks among them. Cover them halfway with cold water and bring to a simmer. Add the ½ teaspoon of salt. Flip the fennel every 10 minutes and continue to simmer, uncovered, for about 30 minutes, or until the fennel is fully tender when poked with a paring knife in the thickest area. Feel free to add a little water, if necessary, as the pan shouldn't go dry before the fennel is tender. To caramelize, add the liqueur, oil, honey, and vinegar as well as the reserved fronds and sauté over medium-high heat. Rotate the fennel carefully without breaking it, to brown on all sides, but be careful not to burn it. Remove the fennel from the pan but reserve this pan to finish cooking the duck.

Preheat another nonstick pan over low heat for the duck, and preheat the oven to 250°F (120°C). Trim the silver skin from the bottom of the breasts and score an even grid pattern into the skin with the score marks as close together as possible.

Place the breasts skin-side down in the pan with no extra oil added and start rendering the fat. If you're using fatty ducks, you should pour off the excess fat every 3 minutes to avoid splattering all over your cooking area. There is no specific time guideline for rendering the fat from the skin and browning it, as ducks have such varying amounts of fat, and people's taste varies for how much fat to leave on the breast. Just continue cooking the skin until it is as brown and crispy as you'd like it (in general, 5 to 10 minutes).

Transfer the duck breasts to the reserved fennel pan, skin-side up, and sear the other side of the breasts over medium-high heat while picking up the sweet residue from the fennel. After about 2 minutes, add the water to the pan to deglaze and then place in the oven for 10 to 20 minutes, depending on the desired doneness (15 minutes should give you a nice medium, where the duck is still pink and moist but not too rare). For the alternative technique, just keep the pan on the stovetop over low heat for about 15 minutes, but you are more likely to get a perfect doneness in the low oven. Touch will tell you the most. The breast should have a tender firmness and the sides and top should have a little give when squeezed.

Remove from the pan and allow the duck breast to rest 5 minutes before serving. Each half breast is normally a good portion, and can either be sliced finely against the grain or halved again into 2 wedges. Sprinkle each serving liberally with the coarse salt and serve with 1 or 2 fennel wedges.

TURKEY BREAST *with* KALE, PECANS & GARLIC

TRANCHES DE DINDE AU CHOU KALE, À L'AIL ET AUX PÉCANS

In spite of turkey's revered status in some countries for Thanksgiving or Christmas holidays, if we're honest we have to admit that it doesn't produce any fancier cooking than the average chicken. That may be why in France it is available fresh in almost every butcher all year round and at a reasonable price. If you can't get a fresh turkey breast, don't sweat it and try this dish with a chicken breast that you butterfly and (optionally) pound flat. This dish may sound more American than French, but since turkey is so common here, and kale has found a footing as a trendy vegetable in France, why not say it's avant-garde French? The use of pecans is another nod to the amicable relationship with America that goes back centuries, but other nuts can work equally well.

Serves 6

6 to 12 leaves green kale (6 ounces/
    168 g), any medium to large ribs
    removed

2 tablespoons (30 ml) olive oil

1 clove garlic

1 large, ripe tomato

1 teaspoon sea salt, divided

½ teaspoon freshly ground black pepper

6 slices fresh turkey breast,
    about ½ inch (1.3 cm) thick and
    roughly the size of the palm of
    your hand

12 pecans, hazelnuts, or walnuts,
    chopped roughly and toasted
    (optional)

Cooking oil, for baking dish

Preheat the oven to 350°F (175°C).

Bring a medium pot of water to a boil. Parboil the kale for 1 to 2 minutes, drain well, and place in a bowl of ice water for 1 minute. Drain well, slice finely into ribbons, and set aside.

Heat a medium sauté pan over low heat and add the olive oil. Mince the garlic, add to the pan, and cook gently; at the slightest browning, remove the pan from the heat. Large-dice the tomato and add to the pan, cooking it down, uncovered, over medium heat for 10 minutes. Then remove from the heat and mix in the kale along with ½ teaspoon of the salt.

Sprinkle the remaining ½ teaspoon of salt and the pepper over the turkey slices. Place 2 heaping tablespoons of the vegetables down the center lengthwise. Top with the nuts, if using, and fold upward like a taco, closing the top of each with a toothpick. The vegetables should still be showing from the sides or this dish will have no color.

Place the turkey in an oiled baking dish and bake in the middle of the oven for about 15 minutes. The meat should be firm but not dry and rigid, so be careful not to overcook, as turkey breast meat dries out so quickly.

ROAST QUAILS with RED CURRANT GLAZE & GREEN PEA PURÉE

CAILLES LAQUÉES AUX GROSEILLES ET LEURS PURÉES DE PETITS POIS

Besides strawberries and raspberries, one of the most common berries to see in the Parisian markets is red currants. They are eye candy, for certain, but quite sour and tannic on the tongue, especially their skins and seeds. That's why they are often made into a clear jelly. If you can't get fresh currants, you could try cranberries, or a store-bought red currant jelly. For the green pea purée, I sometimes like to use some green split peas as well. The color is less vibrant, but they add some nice unctuousness to the texture. Chervil is considered one of the finest herbs in French cooking, with its delicate touch of anise and parsley. As usual with the fine herbs, pass on the dried versions and go with anything fresh: chives, parsley, or tarragon work well, too. Not all dried herbs are to be completely disdained, however: if you're unable to get the woodier Mediterranean herbs, such as thyme, bay leaf, and rosemary, fresh, good-quality dried ones are an acceptable substitute.

Serves 6

GREEN PEA PURÉE:

1 tablespoon unsalted butter

1 (3-inch/7.5 cm) piece white or light green leek

½ cup (45 g) trimmed and rough-chopped celery root (celeriac), or 1 medium-size parsnip, peeled

2 ounces (55 g) dried green split peas

1½ cups (355 ml) water

5 ounces (140 g) shelled fresh green peas

1 teaspoon fresh thyme, or ¼ teaspoon dried

½ cup (25 g) chopped fresh spinach

¼ cup (12 g) chopped fresh chervil or chives, plus more for garnish (optional)

1 teaspoon sea salt, plus more for seasoning

QUAILS:

¾ cup (90 g) red currants or fresh or frozen cranberries

2 tablespoons (30 ml) Banyuls or red Porto

2 tablespoons (30 ml) honey

6 whole quails or 6 halved Cornish game hens

½ teaspoon sea salt

To make the green pea purée: Heat a medium pot over medium heat and melt the butter. Chop the leek roughly and add to the pot along with the celery root. Cover and soften with no browning for about 5 minutes. Then add the split peas and water and simmer, covered, until fully softened, about 20 minutes.

Add the fresh peas, thyme, and spinach. Make sure there is only barely enough water to cover the peas or the purée will be too liquidy. Simmer with the lid off for 5 minutes and then add the ¼ cup chervil and salt.

Purée with an immersion blender or in a food processor and add some more salt, if desired. Optionally garnish with more chervil.

To make the quails: Preheat the oven to 360°F (180°C).

Cook the currants, Banyuls, and honey in a medium sauté pan over medium heat until well thickened. Place the quails in a baking dish. Sprinkle them with the salt and then brush or spread with the currant glaze. Place the baking dish on the middle rack of the oven and roast for about 30 minutes, checking occasionally to make sure the glaze isn't burning. If the quails are getting dark well before the end of cooking, move the pan to the bottom rack. If, on the other hand, there's no browning after 25 minutes, you can place the dish on an upper rack of the oven and roast until you see some nice color.

Serve both the quails and the purée hot, and since there's no sauce called for here, don't forget to collect the pan juices and fat from the cooked quails, and drizzle it on the plate or purée.

CORN PASTA SALAD with AVOCADO, LIME & SUN-DRIED TOMATO

FUSILLI DE MAÏS À L'AVOCAT, AU CITRON VERT ET AUX TOMATES SÉCHÉES

My local organic store carries a good brand of pasta made from corn that keeps a nice firm texture when cooked, and doesn't break up too easily when mixing with sauce and other ingredients like some corn pasta does. Keep trying different brands until you find ones you really like!

This pasta salad is summery in appearance, but the ingredients are available most of the year, so you can make it whenever you need to cheer up your day. This is probably the least "French" thing in this book. But it's easy to imagine it would have its place on the French Riviera near the Italian border.

Serves 4 to 6

9 ounces (255 g) corn fusilli or other bite-size pasta shape

¼ cup (60 ml) avocado oil

¼ cup (60 ml) olive oil

2 tablespoons (30 ml) freshly squeezed lime juice

1 teaspoon sea salt, plus more for seasoning

1 green onion, green part only, minced

2 ripe but firm avocados

4 oil-packed sun-dried tomato halves (dried is fine if you cover them with water until tender)

½ clove garlic

Ground chile pepper (optional)

Cook the pasta according to the package instructions, drain and rinse until cool, then transfer to a large salad bowl.

In a small bowl, whisk together the oils, lime juice, salt, and green onion and mix into the pasta.

Medium-dice the avocado, and sun-dried tomatoes, and smash and mince the garlic. Mix all of these into the pasta, adding more salt and a little ground chile pepper, if desired.

GOLDEN RATATOUILLE with CHICKPEAS & SAFFRON

RATATOUILLE DORÉE AUX POIS CHICHES ET AU SAFRAN

Ratatouille is normally a side dish for meat in many parts of France, but it has so much satisfying flavor on its own. It's just missing that bit of protein found in beans to make it a vegetarian one-pot meal. For a fully complete main course, serve this beany version with some crispy sourdough baguette or a pot of steamed Camargue rice. Ratatouille is already a vividly colorful dish with its traditional mix of red and green, but is rather commonplace in France, with a canned version available in any supermarket. That's why I thought we should go for the gold, using the same blend of vegetables.

Serves 4 to 6

5 ounces (140 g) dried chickpeas, or 9 ounces (255 g) cooked

½ medium-size eggplant

1 teaspoon sea salt, plus more as needed

1 yellow or white onion

¼ cup (60 ml) olive oil

1 yellow bell pepper

2 cloves garlic

1 yellow zucchini or summer squash

1 or 2 pinches of saffron

½ teaspoon cayenne pepper

2 yellow tomatoes

If using dried chickpeas, cover them with a large quantity of cold water and soak overnight. Pour off the water and cover with fresh water in a large saucepan. Bring to a simmer and cook for about 2 hours, or until the chickpeas are tender, adding more water when necessary to keep covered.

Meanwhile, medium-dice the eggplant, sprinkle with salt liberally, and set aside for about 15 minutes. Heat a large skillet or sauté pan over medium-high heat. Medium-dice the onion, add the oil to the pan, and add the onion. Cover. Medium-dice the bell pepper, add to the onion, and cook, covered. Mince the garlic and add. Medium-dice the zucchini and stir in. Continue to cook while rinsing and draining the eggplant. (You don't have to time the cooking of each vegetable. It takes about 5 minutes to prepare each vegetable, so we start with the ones that have a longer cooking time. The idea is to soften each vegetable in its own moisture with little or no browning.) Add the eggplant, saffron, cayenne, and the teaspoon of salt to the pot and continue to cook for 5 minutes.

Drain the chickpeas and stir into the vegetables. Simmer together for 10 minutes while chopping the tomatoes. Discard the excess water and seeds from the tomatoes unless your pot is looking dry. Add to the pot and simmer together for another 15 minutes, or until all the vegetables are fully tender and the sauce has thickened. Ratatouille is not at all an al dente sauté of vegetables, but a fully cooked and flavor-melded stew.

WHITE COCO BEANS STEWED *with* CORN & PURPLE POTATOES
COCOTTE DE HARICOTS COCOS, DE MAÏS ET DE VITELOTTES

The lightness and color of this dish hints at late summer on the Mediterranean. You could make it even more summery by chopping in a ripe tomato. For a light lunch, I'd just serve this with an arugula and Parmesan salad.

Purple potatoes are not some recent crossbreed. They go back thousands of years and have been popular in Paris since at least the early 1800s. If you can't get purple fingerlings, use any firm or waxy potato, but then you'll be missing some eye-popping color in this dish. In that case, again opt for the tomato and maybe some fresh spinach.

Serves 4

5 ounces (140 g) small white coco beans

2 ears fresh corn

5 to 7 purple fingerling potatoes

1 white onion

2 tablespoons (30 ml) olive oil, plus more for drizzling

1 small bulb fennel

1 bay leaf

½ cup (120 ml) water

½ bunch fresh parsley

½ bunch fresh chives

1 teaspoon sea salt

½ teaspoon freshly ground black pepper

Juice of ½ lemon

Cover the beans with plenty of cold water and soak overnight. Drain, cover with fresh cold water, and bring to a simmer over medium heat. Simmer covered until fully tender, about 2 hours, adding more water if necessary to keep them covered. Drain.

Heat two separate pots of water and bring to a boil. Boil the corn in one for 6 to 8 minutes, and the fingerling potatoes in the other for about 20 minutes, or until cooked through. Drain separately and set aside.

Meanwhile, heat a large sauté pan or skillet over medium heat. Medium-dice the onion. Pour the 2 tablespoons (30 ml) of oil into the pan, add the onion, and cook, covered, for 5 minutes. Medium-dice the fennel bulb and stalks, reserving the fronds, and stir into the pan with the bay leaf. Cook, covered, over low heat for 5 minutes, then add the water and continue to cook, covered, until the fennel is tender, another 15 minutes. Mix together with the cooked beans and simmer for 10 minutes. Cut the corn off the cob and add. Peel and medium-dice the potatoes and add. Mince the reserved fennel fronds, parsley, and chives and add, along with the salt and pepper. Drizzle with extra olive oil and the lemon juice to provide more of a sauce.

LES MARCHÉS FRANÇAIS

FRESH PAIMPOL BEAN STEW *with* GOLDEN CHANTERELLES

HARICOTS DE PAIMPOL AUX GIROLLES

Chanterelles are definitely worth going out of your way for, as they have a distinct aroma from all the other mushrooms. I only look for ones that are easy to clean, not broken up or darkened with humidity. If you can only get dried chanterelles, dice them fairly finely after soaking, to make the rubbery texture less apparent. The dish won't be quite as vibrant with button mushrooms, but you can add both yellow and red tomato or a diced yellow bell pepper if you want some golden autumn hues in your plate.

Paimpol white beans, originating in Brittany are readily available, sold in the pod, from July to November. You can replace them with any small white bean, fresh, dried, or canned; canned beans won't need any precooking. This is delicious with a side of couscous, semi-whole grain if possible. Corn couscous is a good option.

Serves 4

5 ounces (140 g) shelled fresh Paimpol beans, or dried or canned small white beans

1 yellow onion

¼ cup (60 ml) olive oil, divided

1 clove garlic

1 bay leaf

1 teaspoon sea salt, plus more for seasoning

4½ ounces (130 g) fresh golden chanterelle mushrooms

2 ripe red tomatoes

1 teaspoon freshly ground black pepper

2 or 3 sprigs fresh basil

Soak the beans overnight in cold water, unless you are using canned beans, which should only be drained and rinsed when ready to cook.

Heat a small stockpot or large saucepan over low heat. Small-dice the onion, add 2 tablespoons (30 ml) of the oil to the pot with the onion, cover, and gently sweat for 10 minutes with no browning. Mince the garlic, add, and cook for 2 to 3 minutes with no browning. Add the drained beans, bay leaf, and just enough water to cover. Simmer for between 30 and 60 minutes, or until tender, adding water if necessary to keep the pan from drying out. The cooking time will vary with different types and ages of beans. Add the salt and simmer, uncovered, until the water has almost evaporated.

Meanwhile, clean and trim the mushrooms, halving the larger ones. Slice the tomatoes thickly, discarding the seeds and water, then large-dice the slices. Heat a sauté pan over high heat. Add the remaining 2 tablespoons (30 ml) of oil and the mushrooms and sauté for 1 minute. Add the tomatoes and pepper and sauté for 1 minute. The tomatoes and mushrooms should be just soft and not a complete mush. Toss in with the beans.

Trim and tear the basil leaves and add to the beans, adding more salt, if desired. There should be enough thickened cooking liquids to provide a little sauce to hold this all together. Feel free to add a little splash of oil and/or water to loosen up the consistency.

BABY PEPPERS STUFFED with CHORIZO, CAPERS & ANCHOVIES

PETITS PIMENTS FARCIS AU CHORIZO, AUX CÂPRES ET AUX ANCHOIS

This kind of appetizer is in the spirit of Spanish tapas, which are almost as popular on the French side of the Pyrenees as they are in Spain. Crack open a bottle of dry rosé from the Côtes-du-Roussillon near the Spanish border.

You can prepare the same recipe with larger peppers, if you like, but I would suggest adding some rice, couscous, or other mild vegetables because the potent flavors here work better for bite-size appetizers. When choosing your small peppers, make the stuffing procedure easier by avoiding peppers that are twisted or too flattened in shape. Serve these with an arugula salad or mesclun greens.

Serves 4 to 6

12 mini mild sweet peppers (about the size of jalapeños, but not necessarily as spicy!)

1 small zucchini

½ mild or spicy chorizo sausage (4½ ounces/130 g) (use a less spicy sausage if the peppers have some bite)

6 oil-packed anchovies (if in white vinegar, rinse very well)

1 tablespoon minced oil- or salt-packed capers (if in salt or vinegar, rinse well)

3 tablespoons (45 ml) olive oil, plus more for brushing

½ teaspoon sea salt

1 teaspoon freshly ground black pepper

½ cup (50 g) minced fresh parsley

Preheat the oven to 400°F (200°C).

Cut the tops off the sweet peppers. With a small, fine paring knife or simple vegetable peeler, dig out the seeds, wearing gloves if you are worried about skin irritation from certain spicier peppers.

Fine-dice the zucchini, sausage, and anchovies. Heat a large sauté pan over medium-high heat and add the 3 tablespoons (45 ml) olive oil along with all the diced ingredients, capers, salt, and black pepper. Sauté, stirring or flipping this mixture regularly to avoid burning. After 6 to 10 minutes, the zucchini and sausage should be a little browned and reduced in volume. Continue to cook until the zucchini is fully softened.

Use a teaspoon to stuff the mixture into the sweet peppers. Push the mixture to make it compact.

Lay out the sweet peppers in a single layer in a little baking dish and brush them with a little oil. Cover with a piece of aluminum foil and bake in the middle of the oven for about 25 minutes, or until the peppers are fully soft. Allow to cool, and push back inside the peppers any stuffing that may have slipped out during baking. Serve warm or at room temperature.

STUFFED ZUCCHINI *with* FRESH SHEEP'S MILK CHEESE & CURRANTS

COURGETTES RONDES FARCIES AU BROCCIU ET AUX RAISINS DE CORINTHE

If you don't have the luxury of having fresh beans in the pod readily available as we do in France most of summer and autumn, you can of course use dried white beans, reducing the quantity by about one third and soaking them overnight. This recipe incorporates a few different Mediterranean influences. But I generally don't like the idea of fusion food and trying to combine multiple international tastes in the same dish, so let's please not call it that.

These zucchini make a cute and easy-to-serve side dish to grilled meats or fish, or a full lunch when served on a bed of greens dressed in a simple vinaigrette and dusted with some toasted nuts. You can also use pattypan squash for this recipe, but the trick is to find something the right size for an individual portion. The little baby ones are cute, but you'd have to count two or three per person.

Serves 6

1⅓ cups (200 g) fresh white beans,
 or ⅔ cup (135 g) dried

½ teaspoon sea salt, divided

6 round zucchini or pattypan squash,
 or 2 regular large zucchini,
 about 8 inches (20 cm) long and
 almost 2 inches (5 cm) wide

2 tablespoons (30 ml) olive oil

1 cup (110 g) finely diced celery

1 shallot

3 tablespoons (28 g) roughly chopped
 dried currants

12 leaves fresh basil

12 leaves fresh mint

8 ounces (225 g) fresh sheep's milk
 cheese, such as Brocciu, or ricotta

½ teaspoon freshly ground black pepper

2 tablespoons pine nuts, toasted

Cook the fresh white beans, fully covered in water, until tender, or follow the package instructions for dried beans (soak them overnight first). Drain fully without rinsing, toss with ¼ teaspoon of the salt, and set aside.

Cut the tops off the round zucchini about one third from the top, and reserve them. Alternatively, for long zucchini, cut each into 3 or 4 thick pieces. Each slice should be at least 2 inches (5 cm) thick. Create even wider slices by cutting at an angle, experimenting one at a time until you get the best-looking shape and something wide enough to be able to hollow out with a melon baller or measuring spoon. To be even more precise, place the zucchini on a cutting board in front of you, parallel to the counter edge. Hold your knife above the zucchini at the point where you want to slice, with the blade edge facing straight down. If you're right-handed, turn the tip of the knife about 45 degrees to the left. Then angle the knife toward your torso at about another 45 degrees and make the slice. (No, it's not possible for the knife to slip and end up in your belly!)

Preheat the oven to 325°F (165°C).

However you sliced the zucchini, the next step is to carefully hollow them out with a melon baller or measuring spoon while rotating them in the palm of your hand. (If you place them on a cutting board and dig away, you will likely cut through the sides or bottom.) Set the hollowed zucchini aside and chop all the removed inner bits roughly into small, irregular dice.

Heat a wide sauté pan over high heat, add the oil, add the diced zucchini, and sauté, flipping or stirring every minute. After 5 minutes, add the celery and continue to cook. Mince the shallot and stir it in with the remaining ¼ teaspoon of salt while lowering the heat to medium. Add the currants, cover, and continue to soften the ingredients for about 3 minutes, or until the shallot is translucent. Remove from the heat and toss with the beans.

Mince the fresh herbs and stir into the vegetables, along with the cheese and pepper, transferring to a large bowl, if necessary, to facilitate mixing.

Meanwhile, bring to a boil a pot of water that is large enough to hold all the zucchini at one time. Place the hollowed-out zucchini (and their tops if you've used round ones) in the boiling water for 3 minutes. Drain well and place in a baking dish. Fill generously with the bean mixture and place in the middle of the oven. Bake for about 20 minutes, or until the stuffing is heated through and the flavors have had time to penetrate the zucchini shell. Remove from the oven, sprinkle with pine nuts, and allow to cool for at least 5 minutes before serving, or serve at room temperature in warm weather.

PEACH & RICE PUDDING GRATIN

GRATIN DE RIZ AU LAIT AUX PÊCHES

Many countries have a variation of rice pudding, but only countries that actually grow their own rice, like France, can pretend that the rice pudding is a true, traditional dish. In Parisian supermarkets, the Camargue rice from the Rhône delta can always be found alongside rice from around the world. To finish this gratin under the broiler, don't bother with any preheating of the broiler. With preheating, the broiler will of course turn off when the oven reaches the set heat level. If that's when you had decided to place this dessert under the broiler for caramelizing, precious little will be happening until the oven cools down and the broiler turns back on. So, wait until the dessert is fully assembled and then turn the broiler to its maximum. Make sure the elements are red hot before placing the rice puddings under the broiler, at a distace of about two inches (5 cm).

Serves 6

1 cup (200 g) uncooked round semi-whole-grain rice (dessert or risotto rice)

2½ cups (590 ml) whole milk, plus more as needed

¼ cup (60 ml) honey or brown rice syrup

1 star anise

1 stick cinnamon

2 cardamom pods

4 ripe peaches

6 tablespoons (75 g) loosely packed dark brown sugar

Rinse the excess starch from the rice. Place the rice, milk, honey, star anise, cinnamon stick, and cardamom pods in a heavy-bottomed medium pot and place over medium-low heat. Stirring often with a wooden spatula, scraping the bottom to make sure nothing is sticking, continue to simmer gently for a total cooking time of 50 to 70 minutes, or until the rice is just cooked through but not mushy. Continue adding more milk as is necessary, or water, if you judge that the flavor is too rich. The final consistency should neither be too thick nor too thin. Remove the star anise, cinnamon stick, and cardamom pods.

Pit and slice the peaches neatly and calculate how many slices you will need to cover the top of each of 6 ramekin or gratin dishes. Dice up the rest and mix into the rice. Spoon the rice into the dishes, top with an arrangement of peach slices and a sprinkle of the sugar, and then place under the broiler, set it to its maximum setting, and broil for a few minutes, to caramelize the tops a little. If you're in a rush, you can also use a propane camping or kitchen torch, if you have one.

CHERRY, ALMOND & TONKA BEAN CAKES

GÂTEAUX AUX CERISES ET À LA FÈVE DE TONKA

Dax is a city in southwest France from which originates the cake based on meringue and ground almond called the dacquoise. The most typical technique is to make two or three large disks of the batter that are sandwiched together with pastry cream to form a layer cake. This interpretation involves cherries, which marry so well with almonds, baked into individual cakes. Tonka bean is shaved like nutmeg and has a complex aroma with hints of cherry stone, almond, and vanilla. In a controversial law from the 1950s the FDA banned the Tonka bean from culinary uses in the USA. Apparently in very high doses it is toxic—just like every other spice— but let's not start ranting about the FDA. In France it's almost as popular as black pepper, but I'm still waiting to hear of any related fatalities. If you can't get it, use almond extract instead.

Serves 6

CHERRY MIXTURE:

20 ounces (570 g) whole, fresh sweet cherries, pitted

¾ cup loosely packed (150 g) dark brown sugar

¼ cup packed (30 g) ground almond meal

½ Tonka bean, grated, or ⅛ teaspoon pure almond extract

CAKE BATTER:

¾ cup packed (90 g) ground almond meal

⅔ cup packed (122 g) dark brown sugar, plus more for sprinkling

2 tablespoons (20 g) chestnut flour or brown rice flour

3 large egg whites (120 g)

¼ cup (60 ml) honey

Unsalted butter, for gratin dishes

3 tablespoons (21 g) chopped almonds

To make the cherry mixture: Precooking the cherries is helpful for avoiding a soggy cake. Combine the whole cherries with the sugar, almond meal, and Tonka bean in a wide sauté pan. Cook, covered, over low heat the first few minutes, until some liquid begins to form in the pan. Then increase the heat to medium and cook, uncovered, for about 15 minutes, or until the cherries' juices thicken into syrup. Remove from the heat and transfer to a bowl to cool to room temperature.

To make the cake batter: Preheat the oven to 360°F (180°C).

In a large bowl, whisk together the almond meal, sugar, and flour.

In a separate large bowl, with an electric mixer, beat the egg whites into soft peaks. Add the honey and continue to beat until firm stiff peaks form, but before they begin to become granular. Stir a quarter of the whites into the dry mixture, and then fold in the rest a quarter at a time. The mixture only needs to be homogenous after the final addition of egg whites. Do not overmix.

Butter and sprinkle some sugar into 6 individual gratin dishes—I used a 4 x 3-inch (10 x 8 cm) size—or a large pie dish. Place 3 tablespoons (50 g) of batter in each dish and add about 15 cherries, immersing them halfway into the batter. Sprinkle each dish with about 1½ teaspoons of chopped almonds. Bake in the middle of the oven for about 25 minutes, or until the batter has fully puffed up above the sides of the dishes and the tops are browned. Serve warm or at room temperature with any leftover cheery juices.

CRÊPES with STEWED APRICOTS, VANILLA & HONEY

CRÊPES FARCIES À LA COMPOTE D'ABRICOT AU MIEL ET À LA VANILLE

The most famous crêpe in France? The crêpe suzette, most likely. The most popular? Crêpe au Nutella, of course (little surprise, as the French are the biggest Nutella producers and consumers in the world). But since palm oil and sugar make up 70 percent of Nutella, I recommend filling your crêpes with a simple and delicious compote of whatever fruit is in season—in this recipe, apricots.

Serves 4 to 6

CRÊPE BATTER:

1 large egg, at room temperature

1 tablespoon packed dark brown sugar

1 cup (235 ml) whole milk, at room temperature

Grated zest of 1 orange

2 tablespoons (28 g) unsalted butter

¾ cup (90 g) gluten-free all-purpose flour blend for bread or pastry, whole-grain if possible

APRICOT FILLING:

10 ripe apricots

1 tablespoon unsalted butter

¼ cup (60 ml) honey, plus more as needed

1 vanilla bean, split and seeds scraped

Whipped cream (optional)

In a medium bowl, beat the eggs with the sugar, and then whisk in the milk, orange zest, and butter. Place the flour in a separate medium bowl and create a well in the center. Whisk in about a quarter of the liquid to obtain a thick paste. Then whisk in the rest of the liquid. Let the batter rest for 1 hour before using, or longer if you overwhisked to remove lumps. There's no need for it to be in the fridge unless it's a sweltering hot summer day.

To make the apricot filling: Halve the apricots and discard the pits. Cut each half into 4 wedges. Heat a large sauté pan over medium heat and melt the butter. Add the apricots, honey, and vanilla bean seeds. Cook for about 10 minutes, adding more honey, if desired, until the apricots are soft.

Heat a nonstick crêpe pan over medium-high heat. It's usually unnecessary to add a dot of oil or butter to the pan, but you can if you think your pan might not release easily or if you like the extra browning it provides. Pour about ¾ cup (175 ml) of the crêpe batter in one quick motion into the center of the pan. Immediately spread it around as thinly as possible to the pan edges by tilting the pan at sharp angles. The fairly high heat is necessary to get nice browning. The first side takes about 2 minutes, and you should see some browning at the edges. Flip with a spatula and cook the underside for about 20 seconds. Cook the remaining crêpes one at a time. You can stack them all on a single plate with nothing between them without worrying about them sticking together, assuming you've cooked them nicely browned as indicated.

Place about 12 apricot slices with their sauce inside each open crêpe, fold over, and top with whipped cream, if using.

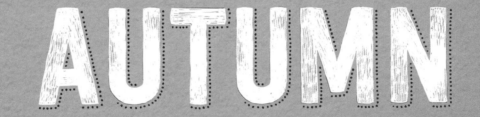

Just when I'm tempted to get gloomy about the end of summer, saying good-bye to all that ripe, juicy fruit and getting reacquainted with gray skies and stressed Parisian drivers, the produce vendors start livening up their displays with wild mushrooms, such as chanterelles and porcini; sunny squash, such as the little potimarrons; and even a fun variety of fruits, such as Muscat table grapes, purple plums, and curvy pears. Black figs are thankfully in abundance for all of October, and quinces make their appearance, lasting through to the New Year. Apples we take for granted, but there are so many varieties and so many sweet or savory dishes for them to be cooked into or eaten raw with, they are really the queens of the fruit world from September to March.

The first cool days in Paris can be irritating if summer was too short or your summer vacation on the Normandy beaches got rained out. But when you've finally given up on any hope of more warm weather in mid-October, it does feel good to get those sweaters out of storage and get that soup pot back on the stovetop. So many things lend themselves to the making of a great soup, whether the heart of the soup is seafood, poultry, or vegetables. It doesn't matter if you prefer creamy soups that begin by sweating your vegetables in golden butter, or spicy Mediterranean soups finished with an extra drizzle of olive oil. You might want a simple, clear broth made from beets and beef bones to start a four-course meal, or a hearty soup to serve as a meal in a pot, made with leeks, potatoes, mussels, monkfish, cream, and tarragon. There is a soup for every mood and craving—and the same goes for stews.

Hit the market in full stride and start filling your basket with something from the onion family, then celery stalk or celeriac, and choose between a root vegetable and winter squash. Next, make a choice among cabbages, kale, or Swiss chard. Decide whether you are in the mood for meat, poultry, or beans. And finish off with some herbal notes, choosing from bay leaf, thyme, rosemary, sage, or oregano, or maybe a combination of all. Your stew is coming together without a recipe!

If your stew was a great success, and your friends cheer your cooking prowess with a clinking of Cabernet, you know that you didn't do it all by your hard work and stroke of genius. When you're back in the market the next day, pass on some of that good cheer back to the vendors that help you get your meal off the ground. When my fishmonger has proudly prepared my sea bass fillets from the best of his suppliers, and I've enjoyed a special gourmet moment later at dinner, I always make sure to pass on the compliments back his way. Same thing goes for the people at the produce stand that bothered to get in purslane and beet leaves even though they're not the biggest sellers. Compliment them on their efforts and not only will they have the small pleasure of sharing in your daily dinner celebrations, but you'll see more diversity in the goods in your market.

Starters

Main Courses

Lunches and Side Dishes

Desserts

LES MARCHÉS FRANÇAIS

WARM DUCK SALAD with QUINCE & BEET

SALADE TIÈDE DE CANNETTE, DE COINGS, ET DE BETTERAVES

In France we can only get fresh quinces from autumn to Christmas, which are most frequently turned into a sweet purée like applesauce. When quinces are out of season, you can substitute apples in this recipe, simply sautéing them in butter for five minutes before adding to the remaining ingredients at the very end of cooking. If you can get quinces but haven't cooked with them before, don't be tempted to simply sauté them like apples and skip the simmering step, as you will need a chisel to eat them! An alternative to using a whole duck would be to just sear three breasts and finish them in a low oven (250°F/120°C) for 15 minutes, slicing thinly for plating. There are some rich flavors going on here, so if you do serve this as a starter, make sure you keep the portions very reasonable. Or make this as a one-dish warm salad for lunch, cooling the ingredients to near room temperature before tossing with baby spinach.

Serves 6 to 8

1 small whole duck (3¾ pounds/1.7 kg), prepared for roasting

2 quinces

2 star anise

1 cup (235 ml) Banyuls or red Porto

2 shallots

4 small beets (about 300 g)

10 chervil roots or 2 small parsnips

1 teaspoon sea salt, plus more for seasoning

½ bunch fresh parsley

1 teaspoon crushed pink peppercorns

1 teaspoon cider vinegar

Spinach greens, for serving (optional)

Place the duck in a roasting pan, breast-side up. Place the pan in a cold oven, heat to 360°F (180°C), and roast for 2½ hours, or until the skin is golden and crispy, and the temperature near the bone in the thickest part of the leg reads 165°F/74°C. Remove the duck from the oven and allow it to cool to room temperature.

Meanwhile, peel the quinces, discard the seeds, and large-dice evenly. Place in a small pot with the star anise and the Banyuls and simmer covered over medium-high heat for about 10 minutes. Remove from the heat before the quinces get too soft and broken up, and allow the quinces to cool, being sure to save the cooking liquid.

Transfer 2 tablespoons (30 ml) of duck fat from the roasting pan and add to an empty Dutch oven or small stockpot. Set over medium heat. Medium-dice the shallots and soften them in the duck fat for about 5 minutes with no browning. Peel and medium-dice the beets, then add to the shallots with enough water to just cover. Simmer, covered, for about 10 minutes. Peel and medium-dice the chervil roots and add to the pot, again adding water, if necessary, to just cover. Add the salt and simmer covered for another 20 minutes, or until the root vegetables are just tender.

After the duck has cooled, pull off the skin and discard. Remove the breast meat and thigh meat from the carcass. Large-dice the meat and stir it into the vegetables along with the quinces and their cooking liquid. Cook all together for 10 to 15 minutes, or until the sauce has thickened. Chop the parsley and stir into the duck along with peppercorns and vinegar, adding more salt if desired. Serve on a little bed of spinach, if using.

APPLE & BRUSSELS SPROUT SALAD *with* SMOKED SALMON

SALADE AUX CHOUX DE BRUXELLES ET AU SAUMON FUMÉ

Many people have issues with Brussels sprouts, which I can't fault them for as they're often served overboiled and mushy as an unappetizing side vegetable. Any plant from the cruciferous family releases more sulfuric odors the longer it is cooked. If you are suspicious but willing to try, see whether you find them more appealing al dente in this multitextured salad. If you just can't bear them, you could transform the dish into a crunchy endive salad.

Serves 4 to 6

½ teaspoon sea salt, plus more for salting water and seasoning

30 Brussels sprouts (roughly 21 ounces/595 g)

1 Granny Smith apple

7 ounces (200 g) smoked salmon

6 tablespoons (90 g) plain whole-milk yogurt

2 tablespoons (30 ml) honey, plus more as needed

¼ cup (12 g) minced fresh chives or dill

Juice of ¼ lemon, plus more as needed

2 ounces (55 g) arugula

Bring a medium pot of salted water to a boil. Trim and carefully halve the Brussels sprouts lengthwise. Lower them into the boiling water, and when it has come back to a boil, set a timer for 3 minutes. Meanwhile, prepare another pot or bowl with the same volume of ice water. Drain the Brussels sprouts and then drop them in the ice water for no longer than a minute. Drain again, finely slice, and sprinkle them with the ½ teaspoon of salt.

Core the apple and slice it thinly, along with the smoked salmon. In a small bowl, mix together the yogurt, honey, chives, and lemon juice for the salad dressing. Place the Brussels sprouts, apple, salmon, and arugula in a large salad bowl and toss with the dressing, adding more salt, honey, or lemon juice if desired. This salad can be served slightly chilled or at room temperature.

LES MARCHÉS FRANÇAIS

BUCKWHEAT PASTA SALAD *with* APPLE & WATERCRESS

SALADE DE PÂTES DE SARRASIN AUX POMMES ET AU CRESSON

This salad is completely inspired by my friend Susan Guillory, one of the pioneers of the whole foods movement in North America, who made a similar one for me while we were sharing a Parisian cooking adventure. I normally find the taste of buckwheat a little strong and unappetizing, so I was surprised to see that paired with the even stronger flavors of raw garlic and watercress, it seemed to find its place. The sweetness and acidity of the apple is a welcome counterpoint to the other less delicate flavors.

Serves 4 to 6

8 ounces (225 g) short buckwheat pasta

1 teaspoon sea salt, plus more far seasoning

1 bunch watercress

2 ounces (55 g) pecorino cheese or a sharp aged equivalent

1 clove garlic

2 tablespoons (30 ml) honey

6 tablespoons (90 ml) walnut oil

2 tablespoons (30 ml) cider vinegar

2 crisp and tangy apples, such as Granny Smith

Boil the pasta according to the package instructions and drain and rinse with plenty of cold water, but be careful not to stir it around too much. Buckwheat pasta is much more fragile than wheat pasta and can break up easily into small pieces. When well drained, place in a big salad bowl and toss with the salt.

Trim off the watercress leaves, leaving only the delicate bits of stem. Rinse, drain, and dry. Cut the pecorino into matchsticks or rough-grate it. Smash the garlic, mince it, and, in a bowl, whisk it into the honey, oil, and vinegar. Core the apples and thinly slice, and then toss all the ingredients together in the salad bowl with dressing to taste, adding more salt or dressing, if desired.

WARM BEET SALAD *with* SMOKED SALMON CHUNKS

SALADE TIÈDE DE BETTERAVES ET DE CŒUR DE SAUMON FUMÉ

Since most of the ingredients in this dish are available year-round in Parisian markets, try this hot in winter, warm in spring or autumn, and cool in summer. Feel free to replace the watercress with spinach, cooked chard leaves, or a large bunch of parsley. The rutabaga can be replaced with turnip, endives, or even sunchoke. I used whole smoked salmon so I could cut it into chewy chunks. If you can only get presliced smoked salmon, add just a couple of finely diced slices for flavor, and opt for chunks of fresh salmon seared separately and left as rare as possible. This will allow the salmon pieces to hold together rather than flake apart, and will keep the salmon moist.

Serves 6

1 leek, trimmed

¼ cup (60 ml) olive oil, divided

2 large beets

1 medium rutabaga or turnip

1 teaspoon sea salt

14 ounces (400 g) unsliced smoked salmon fillet

⅓ cup (21 g) chopped fresh dill

1 bunch watercress, trimmed

½ teaspoon freshly ground black pepper

7 ounces (200 g) fresh, mild, soft cheese, or even drained whey cheese (optional)

Large-dice the leek. Rinse it well in a colander and drain. Heat a large sauté pan over low heat, add 2 tablespoons (30 ml) of the oil, and add the leek. Cover and soften for 10 minutes without browning. Peel the beets and medium-dice them. Add them in a single layer, if possible, to the leek, cover with water, and simmer, covered, for about 15 minutes. Peel and medium dice the rutabaga, and add to the pan along with the salt. Cover again with water and simmer, covered, another 15 minutes. Add water, if necessary, if the pan goes dry before these vegetables are tender. Otherwise, continue to simmer, uncovered, until the cooking liquid has thickened slightly to form a sauce.

Large-dice the salmon and add to the pan of vegetables along with the dill. Heat it through while stirring for 5 to 10 minutes. Just before serving, toss with the remaining 2 tablespoons (30 ml) of oil and the watercress and pepper. Top with the cheese, if desired.

GRATED CARROT SALAD *with* PULLED PORK & RAISINS

CAROTTES RÂPÉES AU PORC EFFILOCHÉ ET AUX RAISINS SECS

This is another example of how you can take a simple and traditional side salad and turn it into a full-protein lunch dish that can stand on its own, like the coleslaw recipe with cured ham (page 126). All you might need is some buttered crusty whole-grain bread to complete your lunch. You could also use shredded beef instead of the pork, or a combination of quinoa and lentils for a vegetarian protein. Replace the tarragon with mint, chives, or cilantro.

Serves 6

2 tablespoons (8 g) minced fresh tarragon, plus more for serving (optional)

½ cup (50 g) raisins

½ cup (50 g) crushed hazelnuts, toasted, plus more for serving (optional)

1 generous pound (500 g) carrots, grated

2 tablespoons (30 ml) honey

¼ cup (60 ml) cider vinegar

¼ cup (60 ml) hazelnut oil

1 teaspoon sea salt, plus more for seasoning

9 ounces (255 g) slow-cooked pork shoulder, shredded (see note)

Baby spinach, for serving

Minced chives, for garnish

In a large bowl, add the tarragon, raisins, and hazelnuts to the grated carrot. I like to chop up the raisins to disperse their sweetness a little. In a small bowl, whisk the honey, vinegar, oil, and salt together and toss with the carrot mixture to combine.

Shred all the pork once it has cooled to room temperature. Mix well with the carrot mixture, and add more salt, if desired. For serving, mound on a bed of spinach, and top with more tarragon and hazelnuts, if desired, and the chives.

Note: To slow-cook the pork, place a pork shoulder roast of about 1½ pounds (680 g) in a covered ovenproof braising dish or slow cooker with ¾ cup (175 ml) of water and 1 tablespoon of olive oil. Bring to a low simmer, and braise over low heat or on LOW for 3 to 4 hours, or until the meat shreds easily with a fork.

BRAISED TURKEY LEG *with* CHESTNUTS, CREAM & SAGE

DINDE BRAISÉE AUX MARRONS, À LA CRÈME ET À LA SAUGE

One of the most popular turkey stuffings at Christmas in France is made with chestnuts. But since turkey and chestnuts are readily available all year round here, I decided to create an everyday dish with the same flavors, to be prepared anytime in autumn and winter. If you don't have access to fresh chestnuts to boil or roast, the best ones to buy precooked are steamed and then vacuum-packed to keep a nice firm texture. Outside of your local turkey season, try this recipe with Guinea fowl or whole quails.

Serves 4 to 6

1 tablespoon olive oil

2 skin-on whole turkey legs (about 2¾ pounds/1.2 kg) (substitute 1¾pounds/822 g turkey leg meat)

1½ cups (355 ml) white wine

2 tablespoons (28 g) unsalted butter

1 yellow or white onion

1 stalk celery

12 ounces (340 g) steamed shelled chestnuts

1 teaspoon mustard seeds

5 ounces (140 g) black trumpet mushrooms

7 large leaves fresh sage

½ cup (120 ml) water, plus more as needed

¾ cup (175 ml) heavy whipping cream

1 teaspoon sea salt, plus more for seasoning

½ teaspoon freshly ground black pepper

Preheat the oven to 350°F (175°C). Heat a wide, ovenproof skillet or sauté pan over medium heat, add the oil, and brown the turkey leg on all sides for about 10 minutes. Add the wine and bring to a simmer. Place in the oven and braise for about 2 hours, turning after 1 hour, starting with skin-side up, until the joint is very loose and the meat is falling off the bone. Remove from the oven and allow the turkey to cool, reserving any cooking liquids.

Meanwhile, heat a large Dutch oven or saucepan over medium heat and melt the butter. Large-dice the onion and celery, add to the pot, and sweat for about 10 minutes. Chop the chestnut meat roughly and add along with the mustard seeds to the pot. Continue to cook for another 10 minutes, to give some light browning to the vegetables. Clean and trim the mushrooms, halving any large ones, and add to the vegetables. Finely slice the sage. Add the water, cream, sage, salt, and pepper to the pot, scrape in the turkey cooking liquid, and bring to a simmer.

Pull the skin off the turkey leg and discard. Remove the meat from the bone and large-dice it, then add it to the vegetable mixture and simmer together for 10 minutes, or until the sauce has thickened, adding water as necessary, since the chestnuts absorb a surprising amount of liquid, and adding more salt, if desired.

VEAL STEW *with* GREEN BEANS & WINTER CHANTERELLES

MARMITE DE VEAU AUX HARICOTS VERTS ET AUX CHANTERELLES D'HIVER

Winter chanterelles are the dainty brownish ones with the tiny stems not much thicker than a skewer. They only take half a minute to cook, which is why this recipe calls for adding them at the very end of stewing. If you can't get fresh chanterelles, don't fret. You can use dried ones, simmered during the entire cooking of the sauce, or any other fresh mushroom. Dried morels also have a great flavor and happen to be my personal favorite, but are expensive and a bit tedious to clean.

Veal rump and top round do not require a long cooking to be tender. However, be careful not to boil the veal, or any other meat that you're stewing or braising. A gentle simmer is always the answer when braising.

Serves 4 to 6

1 pound 5 ounces (595 g) veal rump or top round

2 tablespoons (30 ml) olive oil

1 yellow or white onion

1 sprig fresh thyme

1 tablespoon brown rice flour

¼ cup (60 ml) dry white wine

1 cup (235 ml) water

¾ cup (175 ml) heavy whipping cream

1 teaspoon sea salt, plus more for salting water and seasoning

1 teaspoon freshly ground black pepper

9 ounces (255 g) fresh green beans

1 tablespoon unsalted butter

4½ ounces (130 g) winter chanterelles, trimmed

Large-dice the veal. Heat a large stewing pot or skillet over medium-high heat and add the oil. Brown the veal lightly for 5 to 7 minutes, working in two batches or in two pots, if necessary, to avoid overcrowding the pan. Medium-dice the onion and stir into the meat with the thyme. Cook, covered, over low heat for 5 minutes, then stir in the flour. Add the wine and simmer for 3 minutes. Add the water, cream, salt, and pepper and simmer over low heat for about 20 minutes.

Meanwhile, trim and boil the green beans in a separate pot for about 4 minutes in salted water and plunge into ice water to stop the cooking. Drain and add to the veal for the last 5 to 10 minutes of cooking.

In a separate sauté pan over medium-high heat, melt the butter and sauté the chanterelles for just 1 minute with a pinch of salt. Stir into the stew off the heat and serve, adding more salt, if desired.

SOISSONS BEANS STEWED with LAMB, PORCINI & CREAM

HARICOTS DE SOISSONS À L'AGNEAU, AUX CÈPES ET À LA CRÈME

Soissons is a small city not far north from Paris that is best known for its succulent large white beans. Replace them with any big fava beans. If you can only get dried porcini, dice them fairly finely after soaking so as to improve their texture. If you can get frozen porcini, they can be worth a try. They'll always end up mushy, but some of them at least have a nice aroma. The leg of lamb is a fine cut that doesn't require long cooking, but the shoulder is better off with at least an hour of simmering. You can also try lamb shanks with this, either cooked medium-well for 45 minutes, or slow-cooked for three hours until falling off the bone.

Serves 4 to 6

9 ounces (255 g) dried Soissons beans or dried white fava beans

1 pound (455 g) boneless lamb leg or shoulder stew meat

¼ cup (38 g) brown rice flour

4 tablespoons (60 ml) olive oil, divided

1 onion

1 clove garlic

½ cup (120 ml) dry, full-bodied white wine

1 teaspoon sea salt

1 cup (235 ml) water, plus more as needed

4½ ounces (130 g) fresh porcini mushrooms

1 tablespoon unsalted butter

½ teaspoon freshly ground black pepper

15 to 20 leaves fresh sage, or ½ teaspoon dried

¼ cup (60 ml) heavy whipping cream

½ bunch fresh parsley

One day ahead, cover the beans with cold water. The day of cooking, check to see whether the outer layer is already slipping off. If not, bring the beans to a boil, covered, turn off the heat, and allow to cool to the touch. Whenever the outer skin is slipping off easily on its own, or with a little squeeze from your thumb and forefinger, the tedious task of separating all the beans from their skins can begin—perhaps in front of the TV, or while listening to interesting talk radio. I proposed the job to my toddler, and she loved it.

Heat a large sauté pan or skillet over low heat. Large-dice the lamb and dust with the flour. Add 2 tablespoons (30 ml) of the oil plus the lamb to the pan and increase the heat to high. Brown the meat for 3 to 5 minutes, or until roughly all sides are browned. If you don't have a large pan, brown the lamb in two batches or two pans.

Small-dice the onion, add the remaining 2 tablespoons (30 ml) of oil to the pot with the onion, cover, and gently sweat for 10 minutes with no browning. Mince the garlic, add, and cook for 2 to 3 minutes with no browning. Add the wine, salt, and water. Simmer for about 30 minutes, or until tender, adding more water if the pan goes dry.

Meanwhile, clean and trim the mushrooms, halving the larger ones. In a separate sauté pan, melt the butter and brown the mushrooms over high heat for 2 to 4 minutes along with the pepper. Mince the sage leaves and sauté with the mushrooms for 1 minute. Add to the lamb along with the cream and cook together for another 10 minutes, or until the sauce has thickened. Chop the parsley and add it just before serving.

MUSTARD SEED-CRUSTED PRIME RIB *with* POTATO & CHARD GRATIN

CÔTE DE BŒUF EN CROÛTE DE GRAINES DE MOUTARDE ET SON GRATIN DE POMMES DE TERRE AUX BLETTES

There will probably be an eternal debate as to which type of potatoes makes the best gratin. While waxy potatoes may have a good firmness when cooked in liquid, they often don't absorb the liquid as readily in a gratin, and the ideal is for the milk and seasonings to fully flavor the potato while it retains some texture. It's important not to rinse the potato after slicing, as the starches help thicken the sauce, and you will invariably add extra water to the recipe. The end result is too liquidly and floods the whole plate when you go to serve it. In this recipe, a little cornmeal helps thicken the dish, but without rendering it heavy like a béchamel sauce.

Serves 4

PRIME RIB:

2 tablespoons minced parsley

2 tablespoons (22 g) mustard seeds

2 tablespoons (14 g) mild paprika

1 tablespoon coarsely ground black pepper

1 tablespoon coarse sea salt

3 tablespoons (45 ml) olive oil

1¾ pound (795 g) bone-in prime rib

Fleur de sel or flaky sea salt, for serving

POTATO GRATIN:

3 cups (710 ml) whole milk, plus more as needed

1 bay leaf

1 clove garlic, minced

1 teaspoon sea salt, plus more as needed

½ teaspoon finely ground black pepper

1 bunch Swiss chard, leaves and stems

¼ cup (30 g) fine cornmeal

4 large nonwaxy potatoes, such as Bintje or russet

2 tablespoons (28 g) unsalted butter, for gratin dish

3 ounces (85 g) soft, unripened cow's milk cheese with character, such as Reblochon, plus more, if desired

To make the prime rib: Mix the parsley, mustard seeds, paprika, pepper, salt, and oil in a small bowl to form a paste. Rub onto surface of the prime rib, cover with plastic wrap, and allow to marinate in the refrigerator for 4 to 8 hours.

To make the gratin: In a large pot, bring the milk, bay leaf, garlic, salt, and pepper to a simmer over medium heat. Meanwhile, mince the chard stems, reserving the leaves. When the milk has come to a boil, whisk in the chard stems and cornmeal and continue to simmer, while whisking, for about 3 minutes.

Preheat the oven to 360°F (180°C). Use a mandoline, if possible, to slice the unpeeled potatoes thinly and evenly to about ⅛ inch (3 mm) thick. Butter the sides and bottom of a gratin dish or roasting pan large enough that the potatoes will come not more than three quarters up the sides of the pan. After gently packing the sliced potatoes into the baking dish, add the chard stems with their cooking liquid, pushing the at least half of the chard below the upper surface of the potatoes. If necessary, add more milk until the potatoes are fully covered.

Bake on the lower rack of the oven for an initial 45 minutes. Meanwhile, bring a medium pot of salted water to a boil and blanch the chard leaves for 3 minutes. Drain and chill quickly in a bowl of ice water. Squeeze out most of the liquid from the leaves and while the leaves are still bunched in a ball, cut them into a rough medium dice.

Pull the potatoes out of the oven after about 45 minutes. They should be tender, but not have fully absorbed the milk. Taste the cooking liquid and add more salt, if desired. Press the chard leaves across the surface and into the milk as much as possible. Slice the cheese thinly and lay out across the chard and potatoes, adding more cheese, if desired. Then continue to bake, but in the middle rack of the oven, for another 15 minutes, or until the potatoes have absorbed almost all of the milk.

Remove from the oven and allow to cool and set for about 15 minutes before serving, or bake this completely in advance and reheat slowly, covered.

To roast the beef, preheat the oven to 320°F (160°C) or use the oven that is cooking the potatoes and lower the temperature. If so, add 15 to 20 minutes onto the cooking time of the potatoes.

Heat an ovenproof large skillet or nonstick sauté pan over medium-high heat. Without adding any salt, add the marinated prime rib and sear briefly on both sides, about 30 seconds per side. When the crust is a little browned, place the pan in the oven and roast for about 40 minutes for medium (or the internal temperature of 140° to 150°F/60° to 66°C), or 30 minutes for medium-rare (or internal temperature of 130° to 140°F/54° to 60°C). Approximate roasting times are 20 to 24 minutes per pound (455 g), but it's always more reliable to follow your meat thermometer, since ovens behave so differently. Remove from the oven and allow to rest for 10 minutes before slicing. Sprinkle a little fleur de sel on each slice before serving.

BRAISED RABBIT with GARLIC, MUSHROOM & LEMON

LAPIN BRAISÉ À L'AIL, AUX CHAMPIGNONS ET AU CITRON

R abbit may taste like chicken, but it does have its own peculiar texture. The meat has a tendency to get dry, which is why it is so often braised or barded in a lot of bacon. And its inherent neutral flavor—not to say bland—needs to be livened up with acidity and some perky seasonings. If your tomatoes are lacking some acidity, you can also add a quarter-cup (60 ml) of dry white wine to the braising liquid.

Serves 4 to 6

Whole legs and saddle of 3 rabbits
  (about 4½ lbs/2 kg)

2 tablespoons (20 g) brown rice flour,
  or your preferred all-purpose flour

4 tablespoons (60 ml) olive oil, divided

5 cloves garlic

½ preserved lemon, sliced (see note)

1 tablespoon fresh oregano,
  or ½ teaspoon dried

2 cups (475 ml) water

1½ teaspoons sea salt

1 yellow or white onion

8 ounces (225 g) button mushrooms

4 medium-size or 3 large tomatoes

½ cup (30 g) chopped fresh parsley

½ teaspoon freshly ground black pepper

Make sure the rabbit pieces are dry, then dust with the flour. Over medium-high heat, heat a skillet or sauté pan large enough to fit all the rabbit in a single layer.

Add half of the oil and brown the rabbit lightly on all sides, being careful not to let the oil smoke or the flour burn. Add the whole garlic cloves along with the lemon and oregano. Lower the heat to low and cook for 2 minutes and then add the water and salt. Cover and bring to a gentle simmer for 30 minutes.

Alternatively, if you don't have a wide enough pan to fit all the rabbit in one layer, preheat your oven to 350°F (175°C), and arrange the rabbit in a single layer in one or two large roasting pans. Layer the garlic, lemon, and oregano, but instead of stovetop-simmering the rabbit, pour the water and salt into the roasting pan(s) with the rabbit and braise on the lower rack of the oven for 30 minutes.

Meanwhile, medium-dice the onion. Heat another sauté pan over medium heat and add the the remaining oil and onion. Soften, covered, for 5 minutes. Quarter the mushrooms and add to the pan. Increase the heat and allow the mushrooms and onion to brown lightly.

Rotate the rabbit pieces after 30 minutes and add the mushroom mixture to the gaps between the pieces. Bring to a simmer for another 20 to 30 minutes, or until the sauce has thickened enough to coat the back of a spoon. Large-dice the tomatoes, optionally removing some of the seeds if the tomatoes are very watery. Add them in the last 10 minutes of cooking, along with the parsley and pepper.

Note: You can use store-bought preserved lemons, if you want, or follow my simple formula for making your own, which will avoid the strong taste of distilled vinegar. For 4 organic lemons, you will need to slice them evenly, discarding the seeds, and layer them around the bottom of a medium pot. Add 1 tablespoon of salt, and just enough white wine vinegar to cover, while taking note of the measurement by weight or volume. Add the same measurement of agave syrup or your preferred sweetener and simmer the lemons over medium heat for 20 minutes. Remove from the heat and allow to cool in the liquid, then refrigerate along with their liquid in a clean jar to use within a few weeks, or use a proper sterilizing canning technique if you want to preserve them for months.

VEAL PINWHEEL *with* OYSTER MUSHROOM STUFFING & SUNNY ARTICHOKE SAUTÉ

ROULEAU DE FILET DE VEAU AUX PLEUROTES AVEC UN SAUTÉ D'ARTICHAUTS

I'm not a big fan of doing roasts or stuffed meats that involve getting out the butcher twine. It's hard to avoid some raw meat's touching the bundle of twine and ending up back in my knife drawer, since I don't have the twine rigged up to the ceiling like a butcher shop. And at the moment of serving, I've always got so many pressing tasks to accomplish that I lose my patience for taking the extra two minutes to snip away all the sticking twine bits from the cooked roast. So, I improvise other techniques, such as rolling in parchment paper like a sausage or squeezing into small baking pans that don't allow the stuffed meat to pop back open. But if you're already tying up your roasts blindfolded, I won't deny you the pleasure.

Serves 6

1 whole bulb garlic

2 tablespoons (28 g) unsalted butter

7 ounces (200 g) oyster mushrooms

12 to 16 leaves fresh sage, or 2 teaspoons dried

Grated zest and juice of 1 lemon

1 tablespoon fine cornmeal

1 teaspoon sea salt

2 pounds (900 g) veal fillet, in 1 or 2 pieces

1 teaspoon crushed green peppercorns

1 cup (235 ml) heavy whipping cream

SUNNY ARTICHOKE SAUTÉ:

5 trimmed baby artichokes (called poivrade in France ; in a pinch, substitute oil-preserved)

2 tablespoons (30 ml) olive oil

2 yellow bell peppers

2 yellow summer squash

2 tablespoons fresh parsley, finely sliced

¾ teaspoon sea salt

Preheat the oven to 340°F (170°C). Put the whole garlic bulb in a ramekin or small gratin dish, cover with aluminum foil, and roast on the lower rack of the oven for 30 to 45 minutes, or until fully tender when poked with a paring knife. Remove from the oven and allow to cool to the touch. Squeeze from the tip toward the root to force out the cooked garlic flesh into a small bowl, and discard the skin.

Heat a large nonstick pan and melt the butter over medium-high heat. Trim and mince the mushrooms and add them to the pan. Brown them lightly for about 5 minutes. Mince the sage leaves, add to the pan, and cook for 2 minutes. Stir in the lemon, cornmeal, salt, and garlic paste and cook, covered, over medium heat for another 3 minutes. Remove from the heat and allow to cool to room temperature, reserving 2 tablespoons separately for the sauce.

Place the veal fillet on a cutting board with one of the ends closest to you. Using a fine, sharp chef's knife or stiff meat-slicing knife, slice the fillet open into a flat rectangle. To do this, you can hold the top of the fillet steady by pressing down with the open palm of your nonslicing hand. With the slicing hand, hold the knife parallel to the cutting board, perpendicular to your torso, and begin cutting into the bottom third of the fillet, at approximately a 45-degree angle. If you are right-handed, you'll be cutting from your right toward the left, and rolling the fillet out toward the left at the same time.

Continue to cut cautiously while rolling the piece of fillet away from your knife, to ensure that you retain a single piece of meat. You don't have to try to cut it paper thin or perfectly evenly, because you can lay the cut fillet on a piece of waxed paper or plastic wrap and flatten it out the rest of the way with a meat mallet. Flatten it as evenly and thinly as possible without tearing or creating holes. Sprinkle the peppercorns evenly over the meat.

Spread the mushroom mixture evenly on the flattened veal, avoiding the last inch (2.5 cm) of the edges. Roll up in whichever direction gives you the longest and flattest piece of fillet. Tie up with butcher twine or wrap snugly with parchment, rolling up the paper tightly on the ends.

Place the veal in a roasting pan or gratin dish with the seam side of the paper down, and bake on the middle rack of the oven for 30 to 40 minutes. Remove from the oven and allow to rest 10 minutes before slicing.

Heat the cream in a small saucepan with the reserved mushroom filling and any pan juices from the veal. After reaching a simmer, blend smooth with a hand immersion blender and continue simmering if necessary until the sauce is thick enough to coat the back of a spoon.

To make the sunny artichoke sauté: Refer to page 83 to trim the artichokes, then quarter into wedges. Heat a wide sauté pan or skillet over medium heat and add the olive oil and artichoke wedges to the pan, shaking it to prevent sticking. Quarter, seed, and then large-dice the bell peppers, add to the pan, and cover. Large-dice the squash into equal-size pieces, add to the pan with the salt, and continue to cook, covered, until all the vegetables are tender-crisp, adding a splash of water, if necessary, to speed up the softening. Add the parsley.

Ladle cream sauce onto each plate, top with slices of veal, and add a spoonful of the artichoke sauté.

PEAR, CHESTNUT & RADICCHIO SALAD

SALADE DE POIRES, DE MARRONS, ET DE RADDICHIO

Mimolette is a hard-pressed cheese from the north of France that is colored orange using an extract of annatto seed. It adds some autumn color to this salad along with the radicchio, as cut pears alone can be a bit too drab, especially if you insist on peeling them. You could replace the Mimolette with an aged Gouda or Cheddar, as long as it's artisanal and not colored with synthetic dyes! Once banned in the United States because of the tiny cheesemaking mites that burrow in the rind before the cheese gets shipped to market, Mimolette is apparently back on the shelves to stay.

Serves 6

6 tablespoons (90 ml) walnut oil

2 tablespoons (30 ml) cider vinegar

2 tablespoons (30 ml) honey

½ cup (24 g) minced fresh mint or chives

½ teaspoon sea salt

6 perfectly ripe pears

3 leaves radicchio

½ head romaine lettuce, or 3 baby romaine lettuces

12 steamed shelled chestnuts (about 60 g)

½ cup (90 g) shavings of aged Mimolette or other sharp, hard-pressed cheese, divided

First make the dressing by whisking together the oil, vinegar, honey, mint, and salt in a small bowl.

Slice the pear into bite-size wedges or large dice, and immediately toss with the dressing in a large bowl to prevent brown discoloration. Tear up the radicchio and romaine, and add together with the chestnuts into the same bowl. Toss about half of the cheese with the salad, and use the rest to garnish the top.

CELERY ROOT, CHICKEN & RAISIN RÉMOULADE

RÉMOULADE DE CÉLERI-RAVE, DE POULET ET DE RAISINS SECS

This dish is one of the only things in the book that calls for a mayonnaise. A good mayonnaise is not low-fat and is not made with artificial thickeners and powdered egg! Vinaigrette is not low-fat, either (thankfully!) because fat is what gives salad its substance, its bass notes. Fat is what holds a salad together and makes it sophisticated human food rather than a rabbit snack. And I don't have to remind you that good fats are integral parts of healthy eating.

Serves 4 to 6

2 whole free-range chicken legs or 3 chicken thighs

½ large celery root (celeriac)

7 radishes

½ cup (75 g) tender golden raisins

SAFFRON MAYONNAISE:

1 egg yolk from a large, free-range egg

1 teaspoon sea salt, plus more for seasoning

Pinch of saffron

2 tablespoons (30 ml) white wine vinegar

1 teaspoon Dijon mustard

½ cup (120 ml) neutral salad oil, such as grapeseed or sunflower

Sliced parsley, for garnish

Place the chicken in a single layer in a baking dish, skin-side up, in the middle of a cold oven and heat to 400°F (200°C). Roast for 45 minutes, until the skin is crispy and there's no pink flesh against the bones. Remove from the oven and allow to cool to room temperature. Discard the skin and pull all the meat off the bones. Finely slice the meat and refrigerate.

Bring a medium pot of salted water to a boil. Trim the celery root and cut into pieces just small enough to fit into the feed tube of your food processor. Using the grating attachment in the food processor, grate the celery root, and then parboil it for 2 minutes, after the water has returned to a boil (alternatively, you can use a box grater). Drain, and chill the grated celery root quickly by plunging it in a large ice-water bath, and drain again.

Grate or thinly slice the radishes and chop the raisins. Mix the chicken, celery root, radishes, and raisins together in a large salad bowl.

To make the saffron mayonnaise: Beat the egg yolk by hand with the salt, saffron, vinegar, and mustard for 30 seconds. It's safer to proceed in the emulsifying step by whisking in the oil 1 teaspoon at a time, rather than trying to trickle or drip in the oil. Once you've fully emulsified the first 6 teaspoons of oil, you can risk slowly trickling in the remaining oil while continuing to whisk vigorously. Sometimes the emulsion will break or won't seem to thicken. Simply put this sauce to the side and start again in another bowl with a new egg yolk beaten with a teaspoon of mustard. Drip in the runny sauce as slowly as possible while repeating the whisking procedure. For larger batches, use an immersion blender.

Mix the mayonnaise (allowed to cool to at least room temperature if you pasteurized the eggs; see note) with the salad, add more salt, if desired, and chill for 1 to 2 hours before serving.

Note: For the mayonnaise, use the freshest eggs, and follow the usual precautions for raw eggs. You can also try home pasteurization of the mayonnaise, especially if you have a spatula with a built-in thermometer, using a similar technique to that in the lemon tart recipe (page 74).

ROMANESCO SALAD with SMOKED DUCK BREAST & WALNUTS

SALADE DE ROMANESCO, DE MAGRET DE CANARD FUMÉ ET DE NOIX DE GRENOBLE

Romanesco is one of those head-turning vegetables in the market. From a little distance it looks like a little ornamental shrub. When you come closer you see that the overall conical shape is repeated many times over with every little floret. The flavor is a little closer to that of cauliflower than to broccoli and the name refers to its Roman origins. This cruciferous plant is an ancient variety and not some recent cross like brocco-flower, but it only started to be widely planted in France in the early 1990s. Like most of the crucifers, it tastes better with bacon! A more elegant alternative to bacon is smoked duck breast, which is widely available in France.

Serves 4 to 6

½ head Romanesco (can be replaced with broccoli or cauliflower, roughly 10 ounces/280 g)

6 ounces (170 g) smoked duck breast

½ cup (50 g) walnuts, toasted

½ clove garlic

6 tablespoons (90 ml) walnut oil

2 tablespoons (30 ml) white wine vinegar

2 ounces (55 g) lamb's lettuce, or other aesthetically pleasing tender greens

1 teaspoon sea salt

Bring a large pot of water to a boil. Trim the Romanesco into even, small bite-size pieces, respecting the integrity of each little floret. Dunk into the boiling water, and after it returns to a boil, set a timer for 2 minutes. Meanwhile, prepare a large bowl of ice water. Drain the Romanesco, place in the ice water for 30 seconds, and drain again. Place in a large salad bowl along with a square of paper towel to absorb the extra water.

Slice or shred the duck breast and add to the Romanesco, along with the walnuts (remove the paper towel, if you haven't already). Crush the garlic and mince it, then in a small bowl, whisk it into the oil and vinegar, and toss with the Romanesco mixture. Wash and dry the greens and toss into the bowl along with the salt. Serve at room temperature as a warm salad, or heat for 1 minute in a hot sauté pan—if you're using greens, such as spinach, that wilt nicely.

LES MARCHÉS FRANÇAIS

CHARRED RED BELL PEPPERS STUFFED *with* RICE, SMOKED HERRING & TOMATO

POIVRONS ROUGES GRILLÉS ET FARCIS AU RIZ, AU HARENG FUMÉ, ET AUX TOMATES

As much as I want to be a proponent of whole foods in our diet, some whole grains can simply be too heavy and fibrous for many people's digestion. A good compromise can be semiwhole grains that still preserve a lot of flavor and fiber, but are not a mastication and digestive challenge: rice fits the bill.

A gas stovetop or barbecue grill always wins out when it comes to charring your bell peppers, both for speed and for the smokiness of the resulting flavor. But all hope is not lost if all you have is an electric oven, as long as it has an intense BROIL mode that will remain on maximum heat for 10 or 15 minutes. If it keeps shutting off to not go beyond a certain heat level, it will take you forever to get your peppers deeply charred, and then the flesh will be so soft and fully cooked that the peppers will fall apart when you try to scrape away the charred skin.

Serves 4

1 cup (210 g) uncooked semiwhole (partially milled) short-grained rice (usually easy to find at organic food stores)

2½ cups (590 ml) water

1 teaspoon sea salt, divided, plus more for seasoning

4 evenly shaped red bell peppers

3 smoked herrings (180 g) or other smoked fish

25 cherry tomatoes (about 7 ounces/200 g)

1 tablespoon freshly squeezed lemon juice, plus more as needed

3 tablespoons (45 ml) olive oil

1 teaspoon freshly ground black pepper

½ cup (24 g) minced fresh chives

Rinse the rice and simmer, covered, in the water with ½ teaspoon of the salt over low to medium heat for about 25 minutes, until all the water is absorbed, or follow your rice package instructions. Remove from the heat and allow it to finish puffing up with steam and drying out, while covered, for about 5 minutes. Then empty into a large mixing bowl.

Char all the sides of the peppers over a gas flame, or alternatively on your barbecue or just under your oven broiler set to its maximum heat. Remove from the heat and allow to cool to the touch in a covered bowl, then scrape off as much of the charred skin as possible with a paring knife and your fingertips. Rinse your fingers as necessary, but at all costs avoid rinsing the peppers directly under running water, to preserve all of their flavor.

Carefully cut off the very tops of the peppers. Use your fingertips to pull out as many seeds as you can, discarding them. Small-dice the pepper tops and add to the cooked rice.

Remove any bones from the fish, if necessary, and small-dice the fish before adding to the rice. Quarter the tomatoes and add to the rice. Then add the lemon juice, oil, remaining ½ teaspoon of salt, black pepper, and chives, reserving a few chives for garnishing, and mix well, adding more salt or lemon juice, if desired.

Preheat the oven to 350°F (175°C). Stuff the rice into the peppers and bake in a baking dish for about 20 minutes just before you plan to serve them. You can also bake it ahead and serve it later at room temperature.

BUTTERNUT SQUASH STEWED *with* SMOKED SAUSAGE & FINGERLING POTATOES

MARMITE DE POTIMARRON, DE SAUCISSE DE MORTEAU ET DE RATTES

Morteau sausage is a plump, gently smoked sausage from the French town of the same name near the Swiss border. It's one of many possible cured, smoked, or brined pork products that have the potential to give even the blandest stewed dish a mouthwatering make-over. If you don't eat pork products, you can use a firm smoked tofu, lots of olive oil, and maybe a touch of toasted sesame oil to finish, but tofu and sesame oil would have us straying quite severely from traditional French flavors. My favorite squash to cook with is the local potimar-ron, the younger specimens not requiring any peeling. It's the densest flesh on a squash that I've ever seen, so it holds up very well to stewing. Feel free to throw in a big handful of chopped fresh parsley or chives.

Serves 4

4 fingerling potatoes (about 150 g)

1 teaspoon sea salt, plus more for salting water and seasoning

11 ounces (310 g) Morteau sausage

1 tablespoon olive oil

12 ounces (340 g) potimarron, acorn, or butternut squash

2 leeks

1 clove garlic

1 tablespoon fresh summer savory, or 1 teaspoon dried

1 tablespoon white wine vinegar or cider vinegar

1 teaspoon freshly ground black pepper

Bring the potatoes to a boil in small pot of salted water and cook for about 20 minutes, or until tender. Drain, allow to cool, and set aside.

Heat a stockpot or large sauté pan. Large-dice the sausage and add along with the oil to the pot. Brown the sausage for 5 minutes over medium heat while large-dicing the squash (peeling, if necessary). Add the squash to the pot and brown, stirring, over high heat. Large-dice the leeks, wash them well, and drain. Mince the garlic. Stir the leeks and garlic into the pot along with the summer savory and the 1 teaspoon of salt. Soften, covered, over low heat for 5 minutes. Then add enough water to come up just under the top of the squash. Add the vinegar and simmer, covered, for 5 minutes, then uncover and cook, stirring frequently, for the remainder of the time necessary for the squash to become tender and for the sauce to thicken, which is quite variable depending on the type of squash and pot size. Before the squash becomes too mushy, large-dice the potatoes and add for the last 5 to 10 minutes of cooking, along with the pepper. Add a little more salt, if desired.

RAPINI SALAD *with* SMOKED MACKEREL & GARLIC

SALADE DE BROCOLI-RAVE, DE MAQUEREAU FUMÉ ET D'AIL

This is simple and rustic, but bursting with flavor and goodness. It could be a warm starter if nicely plated or a lunch main course with crusty bread or steamed brown rice. Use any smoked fish you like, and feel free to replace rapini with kale, broccoli, spinach, or Swiss chard. The way things are going, kale is becoming easier to find in France than rapini greens. Make sure there are no forgotten hidden bones in the smoked mackerel.

Serves 4 to 6

1 bunch rapini (broccoli rabe)

5 ounces (140 g) smoked mackerel

1 clove garlic

5 sprigs fresh dill

¼ red onion

Juice of ¼ lemon

¼ cup (60 ml) olive oil

½ teaspoon sea salt

Freshly ground black pepper (optional)

Bring a large pot of salted water to a boil. Trim the rapini and boil for 3 to 4 minutes. Have a large bowl of ice water ready. Drain the rapini and dunk it in the cold water for 1 minute. Drain again and squeeze out most of the excess water. Cut into bite-size pieces and place in a medium salad bowl.

Shred the mackerel with a fork, carefully removing any bones, if necessary. Add the fish to the greens. Smash the garlic clove and mince it, as well as the dill. Finely slice the red onion and add to the greens. In a small bowl, whisk the garlic and in a small bowl, whisk the herbs together with the lemon juice, oil, and salt. Toss this dressing into the salad and mix well, grinding in some pepper, if desired.

CARAMELIZED APPLE TARTLET TATIN

TARTELETTES TATIN

The legendary story of the origins of this tart in the Tatin sister's restaurant in the late 1800s is worth repeating—except that nobody knows which of the many legends is true. And as for the recipe, the Tatin sisters never wrote it down, so every recipe claims to be the authentic one. The version of the story I like the best is the one where chef Tatin forgot her apple pies in the oven for too long and burned the pastry. Rather than discarding the whole pie, she recovered all of the apple, which was splendidly caramelized by the long cooking. Laying a piece of fresh pie dough on top of the cooked apples ensured a quick cooking of the crust without recooking the apples again any more than necessary. What is indisputable is that the restaurant clients loved it, and by the 1920s the famous food writer Curnonsky was describing it as one of the pillars of classic French baking. Below is a variation in individual portions where the richness of caramelization is guaranteed by making a separate pot of caramel before beginning to bake the apples. You can bake these a day ahead and reheat them gently for 10 minutes, or they will be stuck in their pans because of the hardened caramel. These are great with a large spoon of crème fraîche or full-fat sour cream.

Serves 6

SHORTCRUST PASTRY:

7 ounces (200 g) gluten-free bread flour, plus more as needed

Pinch of salt

7 tablespoons (98 g) unsalted butter, at room temperature

3½ tablespoons (50 ml) cool water

CARAMELIZED APPLES:

3 large, firm baking apples, such as Golden Delicious or Jonagold

1 cup (188 g) firmly packed dark brown sugar, divided

4 tablespoons plus 1 teaspoon (60 g) unsalted butter, plus more for pans, if needed

1 tablespoon (15 ml) cider vinegar (optional)

1 tablespoon ground cinnamon, diveded (optional)

To make the pastry dough: Work about three quarters of the flour and the pinch of salt into the butter with a fork until you have small crumbs, then mix in the water until you have a homogenous paste. Add the remaining flour and incorporate by hand. If the dough still sticks to your fingers, add another spoonful or so of flour and incorporate it fully. Press the dough into a ball, wrap in plastic wrap, and allow to chill in the refrigerator for at least 1 hour.

To make the carmelized apples: Peel the apples, cut them in half, and core (a melon baller works well). On the round side of the apples, cut off just enough of the top so the half apple sits does not roll when sitting on the rounded side. In the spirit of whole foods cooking, you can save the apple peels and mince them finely with a chef's knife. Sprinkle the peels over the apple that is then covered by the pastry.

To make a dry caramel: coat the bottom of a small, sturdy pot with about a third of of the sugar, and put it over medium-high heat to dissolve (without water). When liquefied, stir with a wooden spoon and add another a third of the sugar. Repeat the process once more to add all the sugar, which should be fully liquefied, deep amber in color, and just beginning to smoke—but well before any blackening appears. Off the heat, rapidly stir in the butter and vinegar before the caramel cools. (The vinegar,

if using, is optional but gives a nice tart counterpoint to the caramel especially if your apples are not very tart.) Immediately spoon 1 rounded tablespoon of the caramel into the bottom of 6 individual tartlet pans. If these pans do not have a nonstick surface, it is advised to also butter them before adding the caramel. Place each apple, cored-side down, into a caramel-lined pan and sprinkle each with ½ teaspoon of the cinnamon.

Preheat the oven to 360°F (180°C). Remove the pastry dough from the fridge for just enough time for it to soften and become workable. Dust the countertop lightly with flour and roll out the dough. Use a round pastry cutter about a finger's width wider than your tartlet pans to cut round shapes from the rolled-out dough. Place one over each apple half and gently tuck in the sides where necessary.

Place in the lower third of the oven and bake for about 40 minutes, or until the crust has browned well and the apple juices are bubbling. Remove from the oven and allow to cool for at least 2 minutes, but not too much as to allow the caramel to set in the pan. To invert the tartlets onto serving plates, grab them with metal tongs around the top and bottom rather than the sides. Flip them onto the plates and serve warm.

POACHED PEARS IN MUSCAT *with* CHOCOLATE TUILE COOKIES

POIRES POCHÉES AU VIN ÉPICÉ ET LEURS TUILES AU CACAO

Those who think of dessert time as the chance to finish the meal in an ecstasy of rich sweetness turn up their noses at the offer of a mere poached pear. Memories of Grandma's canned pears from the pantry may be lacking dessertlike intensity. The most obvious way to reach the peak of pear goodness is to reduce the pear simple syrup into thickened caramelizing syrup and glaze your poached pear with it. You can substitute other whole baking spices for the star anise. Muscat wine is a popular sweet wine in the South of France with a more fragrant aroma than many other sweet wines, but if it's not available where you live, you could even use a nondessert wine, such as pinot gris or Gewürztraminer, and just add more agave syrup if you want more sweetness.

Serves 6

6 firm but ripe pears

1 (750 ml) bottle Muscat or white Porto
  wine

¾ cup (175 ml) agave syrup

4 star anise

CHOCOLATE TUILE COOKIES:

4 tablespoons plus 1 teaspoon (60 g)
  unsalted butter, at room temperature

¼ cup (50 g) dark brown sugar

2 tablespoons (30 g) unsweetened
  cocoa powder

Pinch of salt

1 large egg white

2 tablespoons (30 g) gluten-free bread
  flour

Sliced almonds (optional)

Choose only nicely ripened pears in season that have a little give to the touch. Hold the pear in the palm of your hand with the stem away from you, and peel from the stem to the base without accidentally knocking off the stem. Remove the seeds through the bottom, using a vegetable peeler or grapefruit spoon.

Lay the pears on their sides in a pot just wide enough to hold them all in a single layer. Add the Muscat, agave syrup, and star anise, plus just enough water to cover the pears, and bring to a simmer over medium heat. Cover with a circle of parchment paper or a light lid that is too small for the diameter of the pot and thus rests on the pears. Simmer for about 10 minutes and then remove this lid before the pears get so soft that it starts to crush them. Depending on the size and ripeness of the pears, continue to cook for another 5 to 10 minutes, and remove from the heat when you can easily insert a paring knife through the top of a pear, but well before the pears turn completely soft and mushy. The ideal is for the pears to remain a little firm so you can let them cool in the poaching liquid and continue to absorb the flavors. Otherwise, remove from the poaching liquid, and when both have cooled to room temperature, place them back together.

To obtain the most flavorful pears, leave them at least 8 hours in the poaching liquid, at room temperature or refrigerated. Then, reserving the pears, reduce the cooking liquid over medium-high heat in a wide saucepan until syrupy. The amount of time necessary for this is quite variable due to variations in pan size and type of stovetop. Use a spatula to push all the syrup into a small bowl and drizzle over the pears when plating. If your pears don't want to sit flat on the plate, feel free to trim their bottoms a little.

To make the tuile cookies: Preheat the broiler to 400°F (200°C), with convection, if possible. In a bowl, use a small whisk or fork to mix the butter with the sugar, cocoa powder, and salt. Beat in the egg white, and then stir in the flour to form a paste. Spoon onto an ungreased nonstick cookie sheet, 1 rounded teaspoon per cookie, swirling in circular motions with the back of a teaspoon until thin and even. The diameter should be about 3 inches (7.5 cm), so on a large cookie sheet you will only be able to fit 9 cookies at a time (you should get 18 to 20 cookies total). If you're unsure of the cookie size and thickness, you can do just 1 cookie first as a test, since they bake so quickly. If you only have one pan, you'll have to cool it down and wipe it with a paper towel before you move on to the next set of cookies. Optionally, sprinkle the cookies with sliced almonds. Bake them just under the top oven broiler for about 2 minutes, or until just starting to brown. Remove from the pan while warm with a thin spatula and allow to cool on a flat surface or a cooling rack. To serve, either prop up a cookie against a pear or lay it down beside it.

CRÈME BRÛLÉE with LAVENDER INFUSION

CRÈMES BRÛLÉS À LA LAVANDE

On my honeymoon back in 2004, we began at the villa of my wife's aunt, up from the Riviera coast in Grasse, the French capital of fragrance. There were huge lavender plants on the property and it was impossible not to be enamored of the beauty of the flowers and their aroma. Many people associate it only with soap, but I think it pairs perfectly with cream and honey. Crème brûlée should be rich, but I find that it's just too heavy with only cream. You'll likely find that a little milk lightens it up ideally, but you still have to jog this one off later in the day! Optionally garnish each crème brûlée with a few dried food-safe flowers, or some berries.

Serves 6

1½ cups (355 ml) heavy whipping cream

½ cup (120 ml) 2% milk

2 tablespoons (4 g) dried food-safe lavender flowers

6 large egg yolks

⅓ cup (80 ml) honey

6 tablespoons (75 g) dark brown sugar, diveded

Fresh blueberries, for serving

Preheat the oven to 250°F (120°C) on the convection setting. Place an oven tray or pan with 2 cups (475 ml) water in the floor of the oven to create steam.

In a medium pot, heat the cream and milk with the lavender and simmer over medium heat for 5 minutes. In a medium bowl, beat the egg yolks with the honey, just to blend and not to add air bubbles. Strain the cream mixture and then pour slowly into the egg mixture while beating. Ladle into 6 crème brûlée ramekins and place them carefully on the lower rack of the oven. Bake for 18 to 25 minutes, watching closely to avoid overcooking (bubbling) or browning. Open the oven door and give the dishes a wiggle toward the end of cooking. They should be firm and set in the center, with just a little jellylike wiggle, and no bubbles should be forming at the edges. Remove them from the oven and allow to cool to room temperature, and then refrigerate for at least 3 hours, or overnight, covered in plastic wrap. Just before serving, drop 1 tablespoon of the sugar onto the center of each ramekin, and swirl around the dish in a circular motion on a countertop to disperse it evenly. Brown the surface with a propane kitchen torch, concentrating on 1 square inch (2 square cm) at a time. Always move the torch on before any sugar blackens, after the sugar liquefies. Garnish each ramekin with fresh blueberries.

Over sixty temporary markets in Paris follow the same weekly rhythm year after year. The grandest of them cover a few blocks of wide, tree-lined boulevards and the most modest of them are nothing more than four or five stands of the most basic produce or, if you're lucky, some fresh fish and meat. These last humblest of markets have little interest for the passionate cook and serve not much more purpose than *dépannage*, or getting you out of a pinch with a missing ingredient if you happen to live just beside them. There are so many little food shops even in the most remote of Parisian neighborhoods that usually you'd be able to walk for three minutes and get the same products in them as you may see at the little market. Therefore, in comping the list of the best markets in town, I've intentionally omitted the ones that lack any inspiration, to the advantage of the other markets that are worth going out of your way for.

Of all of these fine markets, my all-time favorites are the Sunday organic market at Raspail and the Saturday organic market at Batignolles. The reason is not that I enjoy paying almost double to get my produce or that I endorse only organically produced foodstuffs. But these two markets have such a positive vibe in the air,

as if the vendors are that much more proud to be selling what they feel is the healthiest food possible, and the glowing clients are of an educated and enlightened set that feels that buying organic produce at the market is a religious experience. The organic markets also seem to have the most direct sales from the French farms, as opposed to the wholesale resellers who get their produce from around the world through the Rungis warehouses. Lastly, at Raspail and Batignolles you have the best chance to find unusual goods to spark your imagination, such as some crazy herbs you'd never seen before or all kinds of heirloom root vegetables in winter just when your cooking was getting too predictable.

Note that all markets besides supermarkets are closed from early afternoon on Sunday until Tuesday morning, with no Monday openings.

Market street shops occasionally remain open during the afternoon, especially the fruit and vegetable stands, but many close from 1 p.m. to 4 p.m. Permanent covered markets close daily from 1 p.m. to 4 p.m. Farmers' markets open at 8 a.m. and shut down between 1 p.m. and 2 p.m., depending on the motivation of the vendors.

2ND ARRONDISSEMENT

Rue Montorgeuil market street gets mention because of overall street charm and because it's also nearby a few good restaurant kitchen supply stores. Open daily.

3RD ARRONDISSEMENT

Enfants-Rouges covered market and surrounding market street, rue de Bretagne. Open daily.

5TH ARRONDISSEMENT

Maubert farmers' market and surrounding shops of place Maubert. Open Tuesday, Thursday, and Saturday.

Place Monge farmers' market, and nearby daily market street, rue Mouffetard. Open Wednesday, Friday, and Sunday.

Port Royal farmers' market on boulevard de Port Royal. Open Tuesday, Thursday, and Saturday.

6TH ARRONDISSEMENT

Raspail organic market on boulevard Raspail. Open Sunday.

7TH ARRONDISSEMENT

Rue Cler market street and intersecting food shop streets, such as Grenelle and St-Dominique. Open daily.

Saxe-Breteuil farmers' market, at the intersection of these two streets. Open Thursday and Saturday.

8TH ARRONDISSEMENT

Aguesseau farmers' market, on place de la Madeleine. Open Tuesday and Friday.

11TH ARRONDISSEMENT

Richard Lenoir farmers' market, just off place de la Bastille. Open Thursday and Sunday.

12TH ARRONDISSEMENT

Aligre farmers' market on rue d'Aligre and Beauvau covered market. Open daily (the only daily farmers' market in Paris).

Cours de Vincennes farmers' market, just off place de Nation. Open Wednesday and Saturday.

Daumesnil farmers' market on boulevard de Reuilly. Open Tuesday and Friday.

13TH ARRONDISSEMENT

Auguste Blanqui farmers' market on boulevard Auguste Blanqui. Open Tuesday, Friday, and Sunday.

Jeanne d'Arc farmers' market on place Jeanne d'Arc. Open Thursday and Sunday.

14TH ARRONDISSEMENT

Brune farmers' market on boulevard Brune near the Porte de Vanves Métro station. Open Thursday and Sunday.

Edgar Quinet farmers' market on boulevard Edgar Quinet. Open Wednesday and Saturday.

Montrouge farmers' market in the square at rue Brézin and rue Saillard. Open Tuesday and Friday.

15TH ARRONDISSEMENT

Convention farmers' market on rue de la Convention. Open Tuesday, Thursday, and Sunday.

Grenelle farmers' market on boulevard de Grenelle. Open Wednesday and Sunday.

Saint Charles farmers' market and daily market street on rue St-Charles. Open Tuesday and Friday.

16TH ARRONDISSEMENT

Auteuil farmers' market on rue d'Auteuil. Open Wednesday and Saturday.

Gros-la-Fontaine farmers' market on rue Gros, a small market whose crowning jewel is the stall of Joël Thiébaut. Open Tuesday and Friday.

Passy covered market on place de Passy and nearby rue de l'Annonciation market street. Open daily.

President Wilson farmers' market on avenue du Président Wilson, another home of Joël Thiébaut! Open Wednesday and Saturday.

17TH ARRONDISSEMENT

Batignolles organic farmers' market on boulevard de Batignolles. Open Saturday.

Rue Levis market street near boulevard de Courcelles. Open daily.

Rue Poncelet market street near avenue des Ternes. Open daily.

18TH ARRONDISSEMENT

Avenue de St-Ouen market street near the Guy Môquet Métro station. Open daily.

Rue du Poteau market street near the Jules Joffrin Métro station, where I've started off hundreds of market cooking classes over the last few years at "Cook'n With Class." Open daily.

19TH ARRONDISSEMENT

Joinville farmers' market on place de Joinville by the canal. Open Thursday and Sunday.

20TH ARRONDISSEMENT

Belgrand farmers' market on rue Belgrand and rue de la Chine. Open Wednesday and Saturday.

Réunion farmers' market on place de la Réunion. Open Thursday and Sunday.

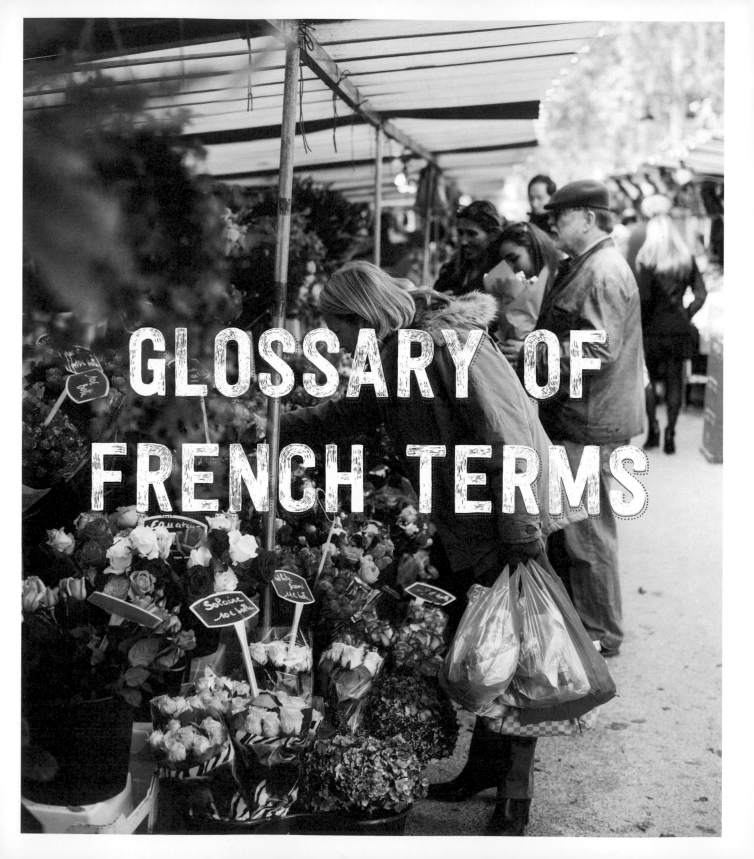

GLOSSARY OF FRENCH TERMS

f you are visiting France and get the chance to shop for food in its markets, there will be many labels and signs in French where you can easily determine the English translation. Other common French terms and expressions might leave you lost, so I've compiled some of the most useful or curious of them.

Abattoir: the slaughterhouse (sorry we had to start with that one)

Abats blancs: from the same root word as in *abattoir*, which refers to killing, the white offal that includes tripe, tongue, and pig's trotters and is sold precooked by the butcher

Abats rouges: the red offal, such as hearts, kidneys, and liver, which is sold raw. Surely you've always wondered about what differentiates white and red offal

Affinage: the process of maturing cheese or wine to optimal conditions, or in other words, carefully controlled decomposition

Amuse-bouche or mise-en-bouche: literally, "mouth amusers," little predinner appetizers normally enjoyed with certain alcohols at the time of aperitif. I prefer to be creative with these and use up little bits of things that are taking up space in my fridge, but if you prefer not to think too hard, my wife will always accept blini with smoked salmon and crème fraîche.

Apéritif or apéro: this can either refer to the time of day when one normally takes the first drink to ignite the appetite for the coming dinner, or the drink itself used to this effect. In cafés and bars, one of the most common aperitifs is kir, a glass of white wine sweetened with a little black currant liqueur. For home chefs, this is an important time of the dinner preparation. Either you're just starting to cook a last-minute dinner, and the libation will quickly get you into rhythm, or you're nearing the end of a long preparation for a fancy dinner party, and you need the apéro to get your good spirits back and vanquish some of the weariness

Annatto seed: although not at all French in origins, used to bring orange color to certain cheeses, such as Mimolette, and to the rinds of certain washed rind cheeses, especially ones made from pasteurized milk and made in a more industrial fashion

Andouiette: pork sausages made from intestines and tripe, not for the faint of heart and which I prefer to eat with my nosed

pinched, or not at all. While I'm an ardent supporter of avoiding any waste of a sacrificed animal, some body parts just carry too much sensory overload to my dining experience.

Appelation d'Origine Controleé/Protegée: "AOC" is stamped on all the wines that have been made in concordance with the official rules for which grapes can be used in which wine-producing areas, and to what proportions, and so on. "AOP" is stamped on all the cheeses that are made following the rules of traditional cheese making, such as using raw milk from only local sources of accepted animal breeds. Many good wines and cheeses don't follow all the tight legislation around their production, but if you're in doubt, buying AOC is never a bad way to go. If you're really dependent on labels, you can find all kinds of other similarly trademarked food products in France, such as chicken (from Bresse) and peppers (from Espelette). AOC is a national level protection, whereas the AOP is managed by European bureaucrats.

Ardoise: has two potential culinary meanings. First, this is used to describe the blackboard of daily specials in casual French bistros where you might be tempted to grab a quick lunch beside the farmers' market. But the literal translation is "slate," as in the rectangular slabs that became so popular for trendy places to use instead of plates, starting at the turn of the twenty-first century. Since it's now the humble bistro that is sporting bits of slate to serve your burger and fries, the new trendy places have moved on to serving on grass or branches, slabs of glass, or edible sand.

Assemblage: the blending of different grape varietals in winemaking. Many wine-producing regions of France commonly produce blends of two to five various grape varietals, such as in Bordeaux, the Rhône Valley, and Languedoc. In contrast, Burgundy reds are known for being strictly pinot noir and most Burgundy whites are 100 percent chardonnay.

Artisanal: in the markets, refers to food products, such as bread or canned goods, which are homemade or produced on a very small scale. Sometimes, however, it's also synonymous for products made in an amateur and substandard way. For example, I usually find the artisanal bread at the markets to be visually unappealing, bland in flavor, and industrial in texture because it's rarely made using a fermenting sourdough starter as in the award-winning bakeries. Bakeries that have the word *artisanal* stamped on their awnings are supposed to be making everything from scratch. But if you wait outside their delivery door at five in the morning don't be surprised to see a truck being unloaded of its frozen croissants or éclairs.

Bar, or loup de mer: sea bass, very popular in France either farmed, wild, or wild and line-caught (the latter being the most prized.) Bar aux huîtres is an oyster bar, or casual restaurant specializing in fresh seafood, white wine, and Champagne, where you shouldn't be surprised to see most of the ladies and gents sporting dashing attire.

Barquette: a small square or rectangular basket, most commonly for selling portions of berries or other small fruit and vegetables. In most markets these are preportioned and you are not allowed to take away from or add anything to the barquette. If you do want a different amount than what you see, you look for a vendor who will select the precise amount you wish and bag it for you.

Bio/biologique: designates organically grown foods in France, and under fairly tight control. Most farmers' markets have at the most only one stand of organic produce. The hardcore organic shoppers take their trolleys to the Batignolles market on Saturdays or the Raspail market on Sundays.

Beurek: not to be confused with *beurk*, which is French for "yuck!"—many markets feature a stand where you can buy a snack of these Middle Eastern phyllo pastries, stuffed with either meat, ricotta, or spinach. These stands are useful if you've decided to cross Paris to try a new market midmorning. By the time you get halfway through shopping and pushing through the crowds, you realize you're already too weak from hunger to continue, and a substantial snack is in order.

Bœuf bourguignon: sometimes the butcher shop will mark raw stewing meat with this designation. Of course, this raw meat is not quite synonymous with the completed red wine stew from Burgundy, but the label is fair warning that you will need all afternoon to cook this meat before it will be chewable.

Boucherie chevaline: as opposed to the normal butcher, this is the one that sells only horsemeat. If you're not sure, it's the stand where only people over age eighty are lined up, or there's no line at all, and there are symbols of horse heads everywhere from the banner to the packaging.

Bouquetière: the vendor selling flowers, which at first seems a very handy addition to the food shopping so as to melt your love's heart upon your return from the market, but in the end extremely complicates the organization of your shopping trolley. You resort to pulling your trolley with one hand and holding the flowers with the other, and suddenly you have no hands free for any further purchasing.

Brocanteur: most markets have a little corner with a few of these people selling antiques or bric-a-brac. It's a useful part of the market for the father-in-law who got dragged along shopping but has no interest in cooking.

Cailles: quails, humble little bird that reached rock star status after the 1987 film depicting the sensuality and artistry of French cooking, *Babette's Feast*. I thank whoever it was back then that recommended the film to me. Probably those scenes of the quails being prepared and the pleasure they procured the table guests sealed my destiny to pursue a career in cooking.

Champignons de Paris: white button mushrooms, mostly produced in China and the USA. Their cultivation was introduced into the Loire Valley in the late 1800s but there has recently been much competition from other countries with a cheaper workforce. In countercurrent, the mushrooms produced in France have kept their prices competitive and stamped the red, white, and blue French flag on their packages, which gives the population a sense of pride and confidence in the quality of the product.

Charcuterie: a shop or stand selling preserved meat products, mostly based on pork, including sausage, terrines, and pâté. If you look for the label "Qualichef," you can find the artisanal products made on a smaller scale.

Chevreuil: venison. The French hunting season begins in autumn, but most of the hunt doesn't reach the Parisian markets before November, and the official season draws to a close in January and February. The hunting calendar is very specific to each type of animal, region, and county. Venison is the most prized game meat and the fillet is about 20 percent more expensive than beef fillet.

Confit: refers either to fruits slow-cooked in sugar syrup, or meats slow-cooked in fat, in both cases for preserving. If fridges were banned in France, we could all carry on quite well (see also *charcuterie*).

Chipolatas: thin little pork sausages sold mostly in barbecue weather

Coques: cockles. Along with bulots (whelks) and bigorneaux (periwinkles), these are some of the humblest items on the seafood platter, the ones that I describe as resembling little bits of pencil eraser. When you see the fishmonger displaying little containers of mayonnaise, it's for dipping these pencil eraser bits inside.

Corse, produits de la: some stands specialize in products from the French island of Corsica, mostly sausages and cheeses. Even though there is a strong anti-Paris sentiment among "indigenous" islanders, and every year there are stories of Parisian vacation homes being burnt, that doesn't stop Parisians from buying Corsican food products, vaunted for being authentic and traditional. (Maybe less now that it was exposed that many fiercely defended Corsican food products were simply using the island as the final stage of production of imported ingredients.)

Crème fraîche: a classier cousin to sour cream, crème fraîche is cream thickened with the addition of bacteria, but because of a relatively low acidity it withstands a certain amount of heat in cooking without being spoilt by curdling. It's mostly used in sauces and soups; you want to use only the full-fat version (épaisse) for the best flavor. It's an easy rule to remember when it comes to dairy products: whether low-fat cream, butter, yogurt, milk, or cheese, they are all seriously missing flavor and texture, so rather than glob on the low-fat simulation, use just the right amount of the good stuff.

Côtes de bœuf: standing rib roast of beef. One of the more marbled cuts of French beef, which is typically grass fed and lean.

Cru: a little word that occupies a large space in French gastronomy, with three meanings: "raw," as in the sense of uncooked meat or fish; "unpasteurized," in the context of the better artisanal cheeses; and "vintage," in the case of wines and champagnes

Cuisson: the cooking, or level of cooking. "Quelle cuisson?" is what the waiter will ask you if you order seared or roasted meats.

Daube: a meat-heavy stew with origins in Provence, with variations on types of meat or wine

Dégustation: in bistros and brasseries, the waiter will say, "Bon appétit," but that's too crude for a chic restaurant, where they normally say, "Bonne dégustation" ("Have a good tasting")

Douzaine: a dozen, for example when you're ordering eggs, figs, oysters, or chouquette pastries

Escargots: snails, most classically prepared in the style from Burgundy with garlic and parsley butter. But the famous escargot de Bourgogne is a rarity that has special protection from the law to preserve its numbers, so the chances are very high that your next French plate of snails doesn't even come from France at all. Ahh, what a world we live in!

Fait Maison: homemade. This seems innocent enough, but beware of things marked "fait maison"! At the stand of products from the Provence countryside, you can find supermarket jams where just the labels have been changed, or olive oil bottles refilled with African olive oil, and so on. Also, "Fait Maison" is a new government-initiated labeling for restaurants to show they're not just reheating industrial food preparations, but there's no inspection and the restaurant owner is the one who decides whether the food is homemade or not. Even if the establishment does have a cook who prepares some meat and vegetables, there's a good chance that the cook is also taking shortcuts with many nasty industrial food products, such as powdered meat stock to make the sauces.

Farce: a stuffing, usually meat-based, for poultry, cabbage, fish, or certain meats and vegetables. The loose etymological connection to humor between the French and the English word is that a commonplace and recognizable food becomes "farcical" and amusing once its insides have replaced with completely different foodstuff.

Flute: in the market refers to the extra-slim baguettes shaped like the musical instrument, for those who like more crust and more crispiness

Foie gras: fattened liver from duck or goose, in France the foie gras is mostly duck except for near the German border. Whole books can be written on foie gras, either strictly recipes or even just the history and animal rights debate over the morality of force feeding. The odd foie gras producer is making the effort to fatten his birds without force feeding, but it's going to take a few decades to make a serious change, it would appear. For a replication of the flavor, take a normal duck liver and cook it to 130°F (54°C) in the same weight of duck fat and purée it all up off the heat with a stick of salted butter and a splash of Cognac. Chill in a loaf pan overnight. (An untested recipe, but I want the credit if it's good.)

Fond: from the same root as *foundation*, this means a reduced stock for the base of sauce-making, from either poultry or veal for white sauces, beef or veal for brown sauces, and fish for fish sauces. If you're not careful where you eat out, your sauce will have a base of some nasty powder that includes a lot of corn syrup, salt, MSG, soy proteins, dextrose, and a little dehydrated stock thrown in for good measure. But don't expect more of restaurants than yourself at home!

Fraises des bois: strawberries from the woods. These are the smallest and most wild-looking strawberries in the market, but rarely would they ever be picked wild from the woods since there is an extensive hothouse production of a cultivated variety of these berries

Friture: refers to deep-frying. You will see this label beside smelt and other small fish destined to be devoured whole after breading and deep-frying. It's a lot healthier than French fries, but the lady of the house probably won't allow you to buy a deep fryer with the goal of frying these up every Saturday night unless you can plug it in in the backyard.

Galette: most commonly, a flat, savory crêpe made mostly or exclusively from buckwheat flour; but if you're in the organic food shop, the term is often used to label a veggie burger patty. If you happen to be in France in January, a galette des rois is a popular puff pastry dessert to celebrate the Christian holiday Epiphany. It's stuffed with almond butter and a little figurine for one of the lucky eaters, who is also then adorned with a paper crown and is promoted to the ranks of the Wise Men.

Gariguette: a common but prized variety of strawberries (there are hundreds of varieties in the world) found in the markets from late spring until the end of summer. It is the recent (1976) creation of a French botanist, reminding us that even here in the land of anti-GMO there has been a wide practice of genetic modification and manipulation. Much of the berry production in France comes from the Loire Valley, with fine soils and a temperate climate with relatively mild winters.

Huitre creuse: this type of oyster represents the large majority of the French oyster production, but it was only introduced into the French oyster farms in 1971 after the popular huitre portugaise was decimated by a nasty virus. Another traditional species, the huitre plate, is quite rare because of susceptibility to very unfriendly bacteria. With the summer being the oyster's reproductive season, they are available in the Paris markets from October to April. Graded with a number based on their weight, the largest specimens paradoxically are given a zero, and the smallest are given a five to avoid further humiliation.

Jus: the cooking liquids (the juice) left at the bottom of the roasting pan or sauté pan after the meat is cooked. Whether you accidentally or intentionally throw this down the sink, it's considered unpardonable according to the tenets of fine cooking. You can carry over the idea to vegetable sautéing and baking as well: if there's some flavor in your pans, make sure it all ends up on your plates. Another reference to jus, being "in the juice," is also a common expression in both French and English restaurants, to designate the busiest period of the service when the kitchen is likely to start falling behind and be under high stress.

Lentilles aux lardons: lentils and bacon is an example of a vegetable side dish you might see for takeaway at the butcher, which of course they had to give a meat flavor. In France, any vegetable that has a chance of kids or adults turning up their nose to, such as cabbage, cauliflower, or endives, is prepared with bacon. Almost anything else that's already considered good without it, such as bread, pasta, and pizza, is also prepared with bacon.

Mâche: lamb's lettuce, among many other possible names for this tender and delicate green-leafed plant, the large majority of which is cultivated in the Loire Valley through the winter months. If you're not strong on French pronunciation, you may want to note that there's no accent on the *e* and therefore this is pronounced mostly like the old TV show or like something you do to a potato.

Magret de canard: the duck breast that by law can only come from the specially fattened ducks used in foie gras production. If you don't like the idea of force-fed ducks, you will have to content yourself with filet de canard, which is also less expensive.

Maraicher: the produce farmer at the market. For the real deal, look for a banner behind the stand advertising the farm name and address, and for a rather small variety of produce often with clumps of dirt still clinging to it, sold by equally ruddy-looking and weather-beaten peasants. These days, the majority of the nonorganic market stands are run by urban-dwelling resellers who try to have a little bit of everything on offer and aren't afraid to sell out-of-season produce from all corners of the globe.

Merguez: often sold side by side with chipolatas, it is a sausage also destined for the barbecue but based on beef or mutton with spices and originating in North Africa. It's illegal in France to sneak pork into a merguez, and it has become slang for a car that has been tampered with to disguise its origins or damages from an accident.

Morue: one of the French words for "codfish," it's usually used to more specifically designate the slabs of salted, dried cod at the fishmonger. Quite common wherever there's a Portuguese or Mediterranean community present in the neighborhood, it's most frequently puréed as part of the traditional dish from the South of France, brandade.

Moules de bouchot: the French are crazy about their mollusks, whether in the form of snails, oysters, scallops, or mussels (a little less so for octopus and squid). Bouchot mussels refer to the tall wooden posts that they are grown on, uncovered when the tide is out, and immersed when the tide comes in. Most of what you see in the Parisian markets is from the Brittany coast,

the harvesting season being from June to January. When you see mussels from outside those months in the market, they are likely to be from Spain, Ireland, Holland, or Italy.

Pieds de mouton: in the autumn mushroom season, you can find these hedgehog mushrooms, which translate in French as "mutton trotters" because of their form. These hold up well in stews and are usually half the price of their more prestigious cousins, porcini.

Poivrade: small, young, and tender artichokes from Provence. They are sold in cute little bundles of five, or when they've gotten old and had their browning stems trimmed down too many times to be bundled, sold individually.

Pot au feu: literally "pot in the fire," one of the most classic and traditional French dishes, from an era where every household had a fire going in the hearth throughout the winter. With certain variations, it's an aromatic beef broth with leek, carrot, and large cuts of stewing beef, served with the broth as a first course, and the meat and vegetables as the main course, the bone marrow spread on bread and sprinkled with sea salt.

Poule au pot: another equally classic dish as the pot au feu, the variation here is that a chicken stuffed with vegetables is simmering in the pot. The legend is that King Henry IV in 1600 wished for all his subjects to have a level of prosperity, affording them the luxury of chicken in their cooking pots. Sunday chicken became the traditional family meal, but the modern take on this dish is to simply buy a preroasted chicken from the butcher just before heading home from the morning's market shopping. Pair the chicken with some French fries from Picard, the ubiquitous chain store of frozen foods, and lunch is served for many a Parisian family

Poulet de Bresse: the only bird sold in France that has an AOC protection (see *Appellation*). This is probably the only chicken you'll ever find on the menu of a fancy Michelin-starred restaurant, usually sold in the markets at twice the price of the regular high-quality free-range chickens because of all the special pampering and treatment the Bresse chickens get in their long and happy lives. Doubling the price does not equate to double the flavor in a plain chicken. There's only so much flavor in a chicken. That's what seasonings are for.

Quart: one fourth, a useful term when you only want a quarter of certain cheeses at the cheesemonger. The smallest goat cheeses are always sold whole, and with large wheels of cheese, you just indicate the size of slice you'd like. Other soft/unripened cow's milk cheeses are often sold by the half or quarter, if you're afraid of that nasty-looking Maroilles but can't resist testing it, you're not forced to buy the whole thing.

Quartier: as in English, refers to a neighborhood or quarter. The markets are really the pulse of each neighborhood, with the most attractive places to live in Paris also having the most diversity and quality of their markets.

Rillettes: fully cooked meat, poultry, or fish that is smashed into tender shreds and then made into a spread or topping, such as tuna salad, by adding either pure fat or fatty sauces, such as mayonnaise. This is very tasty with duck leg, pork shoulder, mackerel, and so on.

Rungis: both a city name, and more important, the name of the wholesale food market in the same city just south of Paris that happens to be the largest wholesale fresh food market in the world. For better or for worse, almost all the food that ends up in Parisian markets and restaurants comes through Rungis, where some 1,400 different wholesalers are grouped together in giant warehouses. You can only get in with a corporate membership card, or on an official organized visit, as long as you can make it to the 4:30 a.m. start time!

Steak tartare: rare, diced, and seasoned beef, one of the most popular ways to eat it in the common brasseries around Paris. You can also get the butcher to grind the meat for you, but at the markets this isn't common practice since there are temperature control issues in the open-air markets, especially in summer. These days, butchers are supposed to be using refrigerated meat grinders, so eating raw meat straight out of the machine is a little less sketchy than it used to be.

Tanins: tannins from bark are good for coloring leather (tanning). They are what your red wine will be full of if it is young and of certain varietals, such as Cabernet Sauvignon. A lot of tannins will make your mouth pucker up but they modify or dissipate with aging, which is why properly aged wines can be so much softer and smoother on the palate. They are also

present in most berries, coffee, tea, and chocolate. The verdict is still out on what precise health benefits these astringent molecules have on the human body. To be on the safe side, it's better to drink just a little red wine, tea, and coffee every day without neglecting dark chocolate cake.

Tarama: a popular snacking spread for blini in France, made from a base of smoked fish eggs, such as cod. Beware of the commonplace candy pink tarama from the supermarket, made with red food coloring and lots of oil.

Terrine: with origins in the word *terre* or "earth," it can refer to a type of terra-cotta or earthenware baking dish as well as to the food actually baked in this dish. Most commonly you see this in the butcher shop or delicatessen, where the food is likely to be variations of pâté, meat, poultry, organs, or fish.

Terroir: again referring to Mother Earth, this word has deep meaning in the world of gastronomy. It primarily refers to a distinct geographical region that shares a common geology, microclimate, culture, and agricultural practices, among other things. Produits de terroir are the traditional or most common foods and drinks from such microregions, which since World War II were often supplanted by industrial goods in the quest for cheaper mass production. In the modern world of commerce and competitiveness, France often has to fight to maintain its traditions. But it's also a very innovative country when it comes to food and wine, and changes in climate and consumer habits will always force the birth of new traditions of terroir.

Topinambour: a Jerusalem artichoke, with no connection to Israel or to an artichoke, since this is actually a tuber (also known by the more recent name, sunchoke). The French term is actually a version of the name of an ancient cannibalistic tribe from the Amazon. In the early 1600s, a group of them was sailed back to France by explorers to be shown off as exotic curiosities, and at the same time, Samuel Champlain brought the plant over from North America. Topinambour began to be cultivated in France, becoming popular under an apparent mistaken connection to the cannibals.

Traiteur: not to be confused with *traitor*, this is someone either in the markets or with a shop who sells premade food dishes to be reheated, most commonly a butcher who sells meat-based dishes and accompanying side vegetables. It can also refer to a company that provides a full catering service, such as to weddings or businesses. The one that you can think of as a "traitor" to the ideal of fresh cooking is the traiteur chinois, which constitutes probably 95 percent of the Chinese restaurants in Paris. They all have the same menu of premade dishes to be reheated in the microwave because the food all comes from the same industrial Chinese food factory. What's more, the flavors have all been toned down for French taste buds, so don't expect anything close to authenticity. If you're stuck at one of these for lunch after you've done your marketing, I recommend the plain steamed rice (about the only thing made on-site) a side of broccoli, and some slices of glazed duck.

Triperie: from the root word for "tripe," these are the butchers specializing in all the offal cuts, which means all the edible body parts that aren't considered muscle. The art of preparation of offal for human consumption comes in and goes out of fashion but somehow the Parisian Michelin-starred restaurants are never biting.

Vigneron: not to be confused with *viticulteur*, which is a more general term for one who grows grapes for eating, juice, or wine. Vigneron is concerned only with the transformation into wine. Much of France's love affair with wine is owed to its Roman invaders of centuries ago. From Italy you can just keep tracing the history of the vine eastward, through Greece, Turkey, and eventually to the southern Caucasus region. But the Chinese have been at the practice of cultivating and fermenting grapes for millennia themselves, although the ideal Mediterranean climate is nowhere to be found in China.

Acknowledgments

From Brian: Thanks to my parents and Wayne, Jenell, and Janice for letting me get away with baking cookies instead of washing the dishes; to Ignazio and Robert Scaletta for letting their delivery driver start making the soup of the day; to Quang for food friendship in Chinatown; to Molly Katzen and Moosewood for their cookbooks and Madhur Jaffrey for the Indian cookbooks and for provoking initial culinary curiosity; to Dean and Dale for helping make my chef's school adventure happen in a foreign country; to David McMillan for bringing me into the fold; to Tom Watt, one of the craziest busboys Montreal will ever know, and without whom I would not be living in France.

Many thanks to Donald and Heather Johnston for the one-way plane ticket to Paris; for pushing me to write a book; for setting me up with my own restaurant, house, and car in the South of France; and for hundreds of warmly shared dinners under your rooftops. Your support as well as that of so many of your friends and family has been very meaningful.

Thanks to Hubert, Michel Maury, Michel Caron, and all the other great maîtres d'hôtel who helped me prep, plate, serve, and wash up while sharing food service wisdom or the joke of the day; to Eric, Yetunde, and the talented crew at Cook'n With Class; to all my students for sharing the pleasures of food and wine in Paris, especially to the ones who claimed they would buy my cookbook if it ever came out; to Giorgio, Stephen, and their crew at La Belle Assiette for sharing a little slice of their world domination with me; to Beata, Aurore, and everyone else who helped me prepare dinner parties around Paris. Thank you to all the local "recipe testers": Dorota, Agnieszka, Gilles, and Grazyna; Ben and Sarah; Roma and Pierre; Morgan and Laurence; Ivana, Zuza and Vincent; and the Canadian recipe testers, which include my dear brothers-in-law and nieces.

Much gratitude to Pauline Boldt, for making it all happen and to her Dave for letting it happen; to all the help from the pros at 26 Projects; to David Tripp at Perseus for initial belief and momentum behind the book; and certainly to Kristen and her good people at Running Press for all the energy and devotion to this project.

Thank you to Krzysztof and Elzbieta and all the Polish family and friends who forbid me from doing any cooking in Poland, and for every time you asked "how's the book going?" and advance thanks to Inga and Klara for all our future joys together in the kitchen and around the table!

From Pauline: Thanks first to my parents for planting the seed of adventure so firmly in my soul, and to my brothers Cliff and Toban for (usually) ignoring me while I experimented with taking their portraits.

Thanks to all the small, quirky magazine shops in London whose product supplied endless inspiration, and to all the independent magazines that I've had the honor to shoot for and to all commercial and editorial clients whom I continue to shoot for.

Deep gratitude to Matt and Geetha Beaven, for opening up their London home to me—sometimes for long stretches of time—for treating me as part of their family, and for being extremely patient while I pointed my camera in their direction. Matt, for his belief in my talent, for his willingness to take a chance on me, for being an incredible creative force and inspiration, and for introducing me to Harry and Jonathan. My dear friend Geetha, your strength of character is undeniable. Your friendship I hold near to my heart. I hope we grow old living next to each other.

Many thanks to two of the great photographers of our time, who changed the course of my career: Harry Borden and Jonathan Gregson; Harry, I learnt more from you the first day we met driving through the city on our way to the Gherkin building for a shoot, than in any classroom or otherwise. Jonathan, your warm spirit and bright smile won me over immediately: thank you for allowing me into your studio to watch, learn, and ask questions. I consider myself incredibly fortunate to call you both my friends.

Thank you to Will Robinson, from Stem Agency, for saying yes to a meeting with me to review my first portfolio, and then for every meeting since. Your critique and encouragement have made me better and your friendship I value to this day.

Thank you to my friends Tina Jones and Marisa Curatolo, for forming our group of three and traveling the globe in search of beautiful backdrops and inspirational produce. Tina, thank you for opening up your family home in Tuscany so we could experiment with food and wine, and for showing me a different side of Paris. Marisa, thank you for making the job of shooting your food so easy.

I am forever grateful to my team at 26 Projects, who have been along for the ride since the beginning when publishing a cookbook was just a crazy idea. Thank you for your support and willingness to hold down the fort while I traveled for weeks at a time; for your creative energy and input into the manuscript; for your patience while I kept adding and tweaking.

Thanks to my longtime friend, Verena. You have been with me through it all, and I couldn't imagine doing life without you.

Thank you, Brian, for being open and willing to hear me out, for saying yes to this idea, for driving me to and from the train station and airport, for cooking the most amazing food I have ever tasted, and for being such a wonderful friend and co-author. To Olenka and the girls, thank you for sharing Brian with me and for giving me a place to rest my head. To Kristen and her team at Running Press for reading our manuscript and wanting to be part of the vision.

Lastly, thanks go to my wonderful family David and Tula. It is because of you that I am here today.

Index

Note: Page references in *italics* indicate photographs.

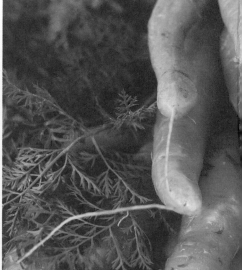

31901060512151